Praise for

CHASING THE GATOR

"Isaac Toups grew up in deep Cajun country. He has been steeped in Cajun traditions his whole life—it's in his blood, and that's evident as soon as you meet him . . . Isaac's rustic and decadent Cajun dishes take you on a journey through places in Louisiana that most tourists never get to see or experience."
—From the Foreword by Emeril Lagasse

"*Chasing the Gator* should come with a warning: do not read hungry. Isaac Toups' colorful tribute to the traditions of Cajun cooking is dangerously appetite-inducing and equally enlightening. You may have to ice your arm after all the roux stirring, but you'll walk away with a profound appreciation for the Cajun way of life—a delicious and authentic piece of American culture."
—Danny Meyer,
CEO of Union Square Hospitality Group,
founder of Shake Shack, and
author of *Setting the Table*

"If you were to blindfold me and serve me some of Isaac Toups' food, first of all I'd wonder what the heck kind of shenanigans you were pulling, but I'd know exactly whose dishes they were. Isaac's food tastes so unmistakably of a place and of a tradition and of a reverence for both of those things, inextricably bound by an exceptional generosity of spirit. This man knows how to raise hell in all the best ways, and the trip there—at his restaurants and in this book—is something close to heaven every step of the way."
—Kat Kinsman,
senior food and drinks editor,
Extra Crispy

"It's hard not to be charmed by Isaac Toups, and almost impossible not to fall for the bold, brave, and unabashedly rich flavors of his Louisiana kitchens. With *Chasing the Gator,* Toups spills all his magical cooking secrets and time-honored traditions, showing how to make everything from the perfect boudin to his daddy's famous seafood gumbo. It's a lip-smacking wild ride through the heart of Cajun country, and there's no better chef I would want as my guide!"
—Gail Simmons, food expert, TV host,
and coauthor of *Bringing It Home*

"*Chasing the Gator* is the Cajun bible. Its recipes are everything you need to live life like a local—including the attitude. If you can't live in New Orleans, cooking Isaac's way might just be the next best thing. And he really knows his way around a pigskin."
—Archie Manning

"Toups' form of authentic Cajun cooking comes at you extra-bold and spicy, like a cat-5 hurricane out of the Gulf. And yet his recipes in *Chasing the Gator* are approachable and enabling. This cookbook is a riveting read, and anyone interested in the heritage of the American South needs to own this beautifully rendered dive into grattons, frissoure, boudin, café au lait, and roux p . . . most soul-stirring g . . .

James Beard A . . .
The L . . . : Charleston Kitchen

"Isaac Toups gives me hope for the future of Cajun cooking."
—James Carville, the Ragin' Cajun

D1201901

CHASING
THE
GATOR

CHASING THE GATOR

ISAAC TOUPS AND THE NEW CAJUN COOKING

Isaac Toups and **Jennifer V. Cole**

Photography by **Denny Culbert**

LITTLE, BROWN AND COMPANY

NEW YORK | BOSTON | LONDON

LIVINGSTON PUBLIC LIBRARY
10 Robert Harp Drive
Livingston, NJ 07039

Copyright © 2018 by Isaac Toups
Foreword copyright © 2018 by Emeril Lagasse

Hachette Book Group supports the right to free expression and the value of copyright. The purpose of copyright is to encourage writers and artists to produce the creative works that enrich our culture.

The scanning, uploading, and distribution of this book without permission is a theft of the author's intellectual property. If you would like permission to use material from the book (other than for review purposes), please contact permissions@hbgusa.com. Thank you for your support of the author's rights.

Little, Brown and Company
Hachette Book Group
1290 Avenue of the Americas, New York, NY 10104
littlebrown.com

First Edition: October 2018

Little, Brown and Company is a division of Hachette Book Group, Inc. The Little, Brown name and logo are trademarks of Hachette Book Group, Inc.

The publisher is not responsible for websites (or their content) that are not owned by the publisher.

The Hachette Speakers Bureau provides a wide range of authors for speaking events. To find out more, go to hachettespeakersbureau.com or call (866) 376-6591.

Photography by Denny Culbert
Interior design by Tandem Books

ISBN 978-0-316-46577-9
LCCN 2018933153

10 9 8 7 6 5 4 3 2 1

LSC-W

Printed in the United States of America

From Isaac:
For Amanda
to whom I owe everything

From Jennifer:
For TiTi
who opened my world through books

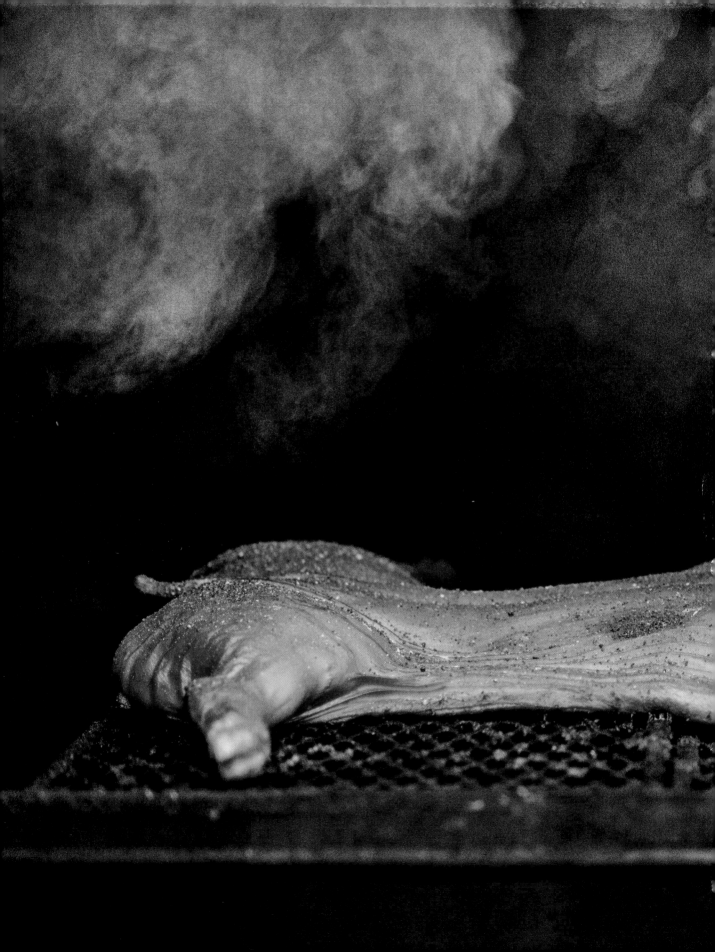

CONTENTS

RECISES

The Fish Camp

The Hunt Camp

FOREWORD
CHEF EMERIL LAGASSE

My love affair with South Louisiana and New Orleans began years ago when I became the chef at Commander's Palace. I have always had a deep interest in Cajun culture and its unique history and cuisine. These traditions of sustainability and community have made a significant impact on New Orleans.

Isaac Toups grew up in deep Cajun country. He has been steeped in Cajun traditions his whole life—it's in his blood, and that's evident as soon as you meet him. His personality exudes his Cajun upbringing. The way he walks, talks, sings, and, especially, cooks brings you right "down the bayou"!

Isaac began working with me in 2001 at Emeril's Delmonico in New Orleans, and boy, could he cook! His creative versions of rustic Cajun dishes were a welcome and harmonious addition to our restaurants, and we quickly became friends. Since his time with me, Isaac and his lovely wife, Amanda, have successfully opened two great restaurants in New Orleans while raising two beautiful children. He was also a formidable contestant on season 13 of *Top Chef*, of which I was a judge.

This book isn't full of trendy recipes. It's full of experiences and stories of a lifestyle that is unfamiliar to many. Isaac's rustic and decadent Cajun dishes take you on a journey through places in Louisiana that most tourists never get to see or experience. He takes you to the hunting camps, fishing camps, the farms, and the boucheries of his childhood. You will slaughter a pig step-by-step with no details unspoken, and you will sit down with Isaac at his table as he tells a few tall tales. You will join his family for a crawfish boil and learn the *do*s and definite *don't*s of enjoying crawfish. Isaac does it all while cracking jokes and displaying an extremely large chef's knife that he keeps in a leather sheath strapped to his side at all times.

This colorful and talented chef gives us a sense of the true Cajun spirit. This book is a testament to his culture, his roots, and his passion for sharing them with the world. His kicked-up versions of recipes saluting Cajun cuisine are noteworthy not only in New Orleans but in America.

These recipes are not overly complicated and they certainly are not pretentious—they embody Isaac's vibrant and family-focused world. They are approachable yet full of ingredients indigenous to his place, and they perfectly represent the farmers and fishermen and wonderful people who are proudly Cajun. From vegetables, sausage, and shrimp to frog legs, duck gumbo, and headcheese, there are recipes in this book for everyone. I don't doubt that after reading this book you'll be dusting off your cast iron pots, calling up your friends and family, filling the ice chest, turning up the music, and throwing down just like the Cajuns do.

Isaac was the fan favorite and finalist on *Top Chef* for a reason. His animated personality, unadulterated talent, and dedication to his craft will certainly take him to massive heights. I am proud to call him a friend and colleague. To this day, Isaac's cracklins and couvillion are the best I've tasted! I can't wait to see what he has in store for us next. Enjoy this terrific book!

My name is Isaac Toups, and I am 100 percent Cajun, born and braised. I come from a land of swamps and cypress trees, of hunting land surrounded by forests and bayous packed with fish. I grew up in Rayne, Louisiana, a tiny town of about 8,000 people in Acadia Parish, deep in the heart of Cajun country.

My people go back far here—really far. My family members first showed up in the Atchafalaya Basin in the 1700s.

We never do anything small, and backyard gatherings of a couple dozen people are just your average Saturday afternoon. Here, you'll find boudin, cracklins, and gumbo so damn good it might make you cry. And if you do, that'd be alright. We truly live to eat. That's the approach I bring to my restaurants, Toups' Meatery and Toups South, in New Orleans—and to this book.

So what does it mean to cook Cajun? Cajuns are resourceful. We cook from the land. We take whatever is available and work with it—crawfish, ducks, rice, sugarcane, nutria rats (yep, we even found a way to make our rodents taste good). We're not rich folks, so our food is all about making do with what we have. Don't have much meat to feed a big family? Make a roux-thickened gravy and stretch it. Want fresh vegetables? Grow them.

We started cooking what we do out of necessity. But then we decided we liked it, and traditions were born. Many of those traditions got passed down; some got lost. And then some got revived, like the boucherie (page 22). Cajuns were going whole hog *way* before it was cool.

I'm lucky to come from both Prairie Cajun and Coastal Cajun stock. Yes, there is more than one kind of Cajun. Most of the difference boils down to the landscape, and how folks use what's around them. Mama grew up a Prairie Cajun from Oakdale. There, it's mostly land-locked, so you raised pigs, you went hunting, you grew your own garden, you ate a *lot* of rice. Daddy's family were the Coastal Cajuns, from Thibodaux, and it was all about crab, shrimp, oysters, and whatever

fish they could land. (Caught fish is a lot cheaper than bought fish—depending on the price of your boat.) And everybody does crawfish.

This book reflects both sides of my raising, and you'll see chapters broken out by how and where we get together to eat: The Boucherie, The Community Table, The Homestead, The Fish Camp, and The Hunt Camp.

I don't know if I have any of my grandmothers' recipes properly written down. They just had the way they did things. If you asked questions, they'd explain, or you could watch and learn.

But traditions evolve. People come to New Orleans expecting to eat Cajun food. These days, they're getting a melding of the last 300 years of influence: French, Spanish, Afro-Caribbean, Vietnamese, Creole—and Cajun. We borrow from everybody and make it our own. Modern Cajun food is rooted in the old ways, but incorporates ingredients and techniques brought in by our new neighbors. If we like how you cook, we'll borrow it, and after a while we'll call it ours—respectfully.

Sometimes I wonder how far my cooking gets away from old-school Cajun. Is it too far? I say no. "Cajun" is a lifestyle, it's a mindset, it's an area, and it's a people. This isn't the history of classic Cajun food. That's another book. This is the story of a young wild Cajun and the experiences that made me the cook I am today. I cook unapologetically. Yes, the food is brown. But it brings that in-your-face flavor. Subtle, delicate—that's not me. At all. And you'll see I've gotten up to some dangerous antics outside of the kitchen. If you're stupid enough to throw tomahawks, play Stump, or do anything else that might get you hurt . . . well, you deserve it.

Chasing the Gator isn't about cooking alligator tails. It's a metaphor for how I got to where I wound up, and it's about where I'm going. It's about leaving home, remembering where I come from, and using the dual influences of my Cajun upbringing to make my own food today. From a baby cook to a chef with my own restaurants, I've always chased flavor. And I've caught a few of my personal flavor gators. But I'm still searching. I'm always looking for more, for better. That's how I cook, and that's how I live.

Now get the fuck out there and make something to eat.

CHASING
THE
GATOR

CAJUN 101

Boudreaux and Thibodeaux were walking through the woods the other day, when a flying saucer landed near them. A door opened, and two little green aliens climbed down out of the spacecraft.

Thibodeaux turned to Boudreaux, "Mais, look at dat. What you tink dat is?"

Boudreaux, aiming his shotgun at the little space critters, replied, "Thibodeaux, I don' know, but you hurry back to de camp, put on de rice pot, and start makin' a roux!"

How do you cook Cajun? First, think about what it's like to eat the food. We Cajuns like deep, concentrated flavors. Rarely will you taste a Cajun dish and think, "Oh, that's light and delicate." The flavor is in your face—always intense—but it's not necessarily going to burn your mouth with spicy chiles.

You'll find lots of toasted black pepper, white pepper, cayenne, rich stocks, Creole mustard, hot sauce, and garlic here. *Everybody* uses garlic—but nobody uses as much as me. Stews are flavored deeply with the Cajun trinity (onion, bell pepper, and celery) and enriched with roux (fat and flour).

The roux is really the base of Cajun cuisine. Our food is built on making do with what you have, and a roux lets you stretch a dish for not much money. Flour is cheap. Roux thickens your gravy, gives depth of flavor, and can help you not miss the meat if all you've got is a poor man's rice and gravy.

If you master the Cajun basics, you can cook anywhere in the world. Take the local meat, local vegetables, some salt, and fire, and as long as you can locate a pot to cook in, you're good to go. That's why you want a Cajun on your team during the zombie apocalypse. We can make do with *anything*. I mean, we take critters that swim in the damn mud and eat them. Know that big log in the swamp with the big teeth? We eat that too. Ever take one of those rocks that's got a ball of snot in it and shuck it open and eat one? Exactly.

Cooking Cajun isn't hard. Some dishes are time intensive, but nothing is beyond the realm of possibility. The techniques are pretty simple. The biggest challenge you might have is finding certain ingredients outside of south Louisiana. But a chicken and sausage gumbo? Master your roux and you can make that *anywhere*.

EQUIPMENT

Cajuns don't need much by way of equipment. As a people, we are masters at making do with what's on hand. But there are a few things every Cajun kitchen has to have.

A **Dutch oven** is probably the most used pot in my kitchen—and in this book. I like my **Le Creuset**. But my daddy's mama, Maw Maw Toups, used a **Magnalite cast aluminum pot.** Down here, when you get married, your in-laws give you a Magnalite and a **Crock-Pot.** It's like the Cajun dowry.

You'll also want some **cast iron pans.** Cast iron should be something you inherit or pass along after you're gone. If you don't have one, invest in a **10- or 12-inch round pan** for cornbread and **several big pots that hold at least 7 quarts** for stews. And always take care of them, which means cleaning them. At a boucherie or whenever you're roasting a whole pig, throw the cast iron in the fire pit after you're done cooking. It will get red hot. You just fetch it afterward and rub it down with a little oil. Otherwise, wash cast iron by hand (no soap), dry it well, and then rub it down with oil. I use grapeseed oil.

Cast iron is just so versatile. It heats well. It's heavy as hell. You could use it as a weapon if you need to—it could take a couple of bullets and be just fine. You can even use it as a hammer. In fact, I'm sure I have.

To make sausage, you'll want to get a **meat grinder** and a **sausage stuffer.** (Or start developing a deeper relationship with your butcher.) If you want to cook a big batch of my dad's crab stew (page 161)—and trust me, you do—make sure you have a **13-quart stockpot.** For boiled crawfish, you'll want something bigger, like a **crawfish pot,** a **turkey fryer,** or a **32-quart boiling pot with a punched basket.**

Beyond that? Some **sharp knives** and **something to cut on,** and you'll be good. If you need anything else you don't have, just do like a Cajun and improvise.

CAJUN ENGINEERING

Last year, I was roasting a whole pig for a friend's birthday party. But we were up in upstate New York, and there wasn't anything around to cook it on. So we built up a little piggy altar about four feet high with some cinder blocks and got a fire going in the center. While the wood turned to embers, we trussed the pig up real good. There was no spit, no grill top, nothing. So we made one.

I got some rabbit wire and a couple of poles of rebar. We put the rabbit wire down on a picnic table, splayed the pig across, and folded the wire over, like making an envelope. We then threaded the rebar through, with a pole on each side of the pig, making sure to keep our delicious pink friend tightly wrapped.

There you go: a grill with handles for flipping the pig, all in one. We set that over the coals until it dripped with fat. It was magical. And I looked like a goddamn genius.

INGREDIENTS

Cajun cooking is regional cooking. We eat what we eat because it grows here. Beyond that, there are a few basics, like the **trinity** and **roux,** that make up the heart of many dishes. I've got something of a vinegar fetish—I'm an acid freak—so I use lots of **sherry vinegar** and **white wine vinegar** throughout my recipes. You'll learn I really like **grapeseed oil** because it's got a higher smoke point than most oils and can handle the intense heat I like to use when cooking. I prefer **canola oil** for dressings and sauces you don't have to cook. I prefer **popcorn salt** when I deep-fry because it sticks to the food better than any other salt.

The **Cajun trinity** is onion, bell pepper, and celery. That trio, chopped and added to roux, forms the backbone of nearly every sauce, soup, gumbo, or smothered dish in the southern Louisiana repertoire. This is the Cajun version of mirepoix, subbing in bell pepper for carrots, and gets its name from the deep Catholic roots that spread across Acadiana. It's the heart and soul of Cajun recipes.

In the trinity, you can use any kind of bell pepper, but I always use red ones instead of green. In fact, red bell peppers are the only ones I allow in my restaurants. Why? I'm color blind. I can't see red. Couvillion should be red. Crawfish bisque, also red. A green pepper ruins the look. So if every pepper I can pick up is red, I don't have to worry about grabbing the wrong one.

To make trinity, I always use **2 parts onion, 1 part red bell pepper,** and **1 part celery.**

And even though **garlic** isn't part of the trinity, it's something I get almost religious about. I use it like I'm trying to keep vampires away. Hey, it's Louisiana. Anne Rice might know what the hell she's talking about.

Mama taught me to make coffee by putting in a scoop per person and adding one for the pot. That's also my general approach to garlic: a clove for every person plus one extra. At our restaurants we use a gallon of garlic every day, easy, so I rely on giant canisters of **pre-peeled cloves.** When you're making my boudin (page 28) and you get to where it calls for 100 cloves, you'll become a believer in buying pre-peeled too. But stay away from the pre-minced stuff—that's evil.

Blonde Roux

Brick Roux

Dark or Caramel-Colored Roux

15-Minute Dark Roux

ROUX

Roux thickens sauces, adds depth to braises, and holds Cajun dishes together. Half the recipes I know begin with "Make a roux." If you master only one thing in this book, make it roux.

Roux almost always has a 1:1 ratio of fat to flour. Most of my recipes call for ¼ cup of each. You cook them together over medium heat, stirring almost constantly. You'll want to use a thick-bottomed pot like a Dutch oven or a cast iron skillet because you need even heat. The biggest enemy of a roux (other than not paying attention to it) is a pan with a hot spot.

The darker a roux gets, the less power it has to thicken a sauce. I believe that's from the denaturing of proteins in the flour as it cooks, but you'd have to ask Alton Brown about that.

Before you start making a roux, make sure you've chopped your trinity and that it's ready to go once your roux hits the right color.

WHITE ROUX

White roux is just cold fat and cold flour. I don't use it at all. Some old-school recipes call for it, but I always cook my roux. Otherwise, when the dish is done, you can still taste the raw flour—and that's nasty. I'm only telling you what white roux is so I can tell you this: DO. NOT. MAKE. IT.

BLONDE ROUX

This is white roux that's been cooked for a couple minutes. Blonde roux is made with butter and becomes a base for a béchamel sauce, white gravy, cream sauce, or any cheese sauce. Use it basically anytime you're trying to thicken dairy. When I make a roux with butter, I typically deviate slightly from the 1:1 fat-to-flour ratio because the butter loses a little weight when water cooks out of it. In general, it's okay to have a little more fat than flour in a roux. | *Makes ¼ cup*

4 tablespoons unsalted butter   3 tablespoons all-purpose flour

› In a Dutch oven or heavy skillet set over medium heat, heat the butter until it melts and then stops bubbling. Watch carefully; you don't want it to brown. Once the butter's melted, you'll see sediment collect at the bottom of the pan. Those are the milk solids, and some people scoop them out—but you should taste them. They're delicious. Don't throw them away.

› Once the butter stops bubbling, dump the flour in—no need to sprinkle it like it's precious. Stir well to combine the butter and flour. Cook the roux a minute or two, stirring often, until it darkens by one shade and starts to smell nutty.

BRICK ROUX

Brick roux is blonde roux cooked with tomato paste. As soon as you have blonde roux, take the paste (or even tomato puree or tomatoes crushed by hand) and caramelize it with the roux.

I use brick roux mostly for couvillion (page 84), a rich seafood stew Maw Maw Toups always made. I also modify it for my Crawfish Bisque (page 86). Daddy's gumbo (page 170) uses V8 instead of tomato paste for a whole other twist—but he's nuts. | *Makes ¾ cup*

4 tablespoons unsalted butter	3 tablespoons all-purpose flour	½ cup tomato paste

› In a Dutch oven or heavy skillet set over medium heat, make a blonde roux (see previous page) with the butter and flour. Once the roux is ready, add the tomato paste. Stir that in and let it caramelize until it starts sticking to the bottom. Cook it until it browns a little. I smash down the tomato paste evenly across the bottom of the pot to increase the surface area that is caramelized by the heat. This should take about 10 minutes total, and results in a brick red roux with a charred tomato flavor.

DARK or CARAMEL-COLORED ROUX

Dark roux is the stuff of Cajun legend. It's the difference between gumbo and "Holy shit, that's a gumbo!" I like mine to be mahogany or rich milk chocolate in color. Throughout this book, you'll occasionally see recipes that call for a caramel-colored roux. It's the same process, but you quit cooking it a little earlier.

You can use plain-Jane vegetable oil to make a roux (in fact, my daddy usually does), but I prefer grapeseed oil when I'm making dark roux because it's got a higher smoke point. That means you can cook it hotter for longer without burning the oil. You can also use peanut oil or even refined avocado oil (which has the highest smoke point of any oil I've found). Do not use butter: It will burn and taste bitter, and ruin your dish.

If this is your first dark roux, turn down the heat and go low and slow. Settle in and know it's going to take about 45 minutes of constant stirring to get there. Invest in a long-handled wooden spoon if you want to save your knuckles from the constant heat exposure. (Or don't. It's your hand.) I recommend a spatula-style wooden spoon with a flat edge so you can really scrape the bottom. Be diligent about scraping around the edges to make sure none of the roux burns.

Chop your trinity before you start making a dark roux, so you can add it immediately when the color's right. The difference between great dark roux and burnt garbage is only a minute. If you burn even a little bit of it, you might as well throw it all out and start over. But don't cry about it. There's an old saying: "If you haven't burned a roux, you've never made one." You'll know if it's burned by the smell. No matter how dark a roux gets, if it's still good it won't smell acrid at all. | *Makes 6 tablespoons*

¼ cup grapeseed oil	¼ cup all-purpose flour

› In a Dutch oven or heavy skillet over medium heat, stir together the oil and flour. Then stir. And stir. And stir. The darker the roux gets, the more frequently you must stir it. As it nears the color of caramel or milk chocolate, you will be stirring almost constantly.

› The second your roux hits the color you want, add your trinity. This will immediately stop the roux from getting any darker.

15-MINUTE DARK ROUX

Some people say it's impossible, or straight-up heresy, to make a dark roux in only 15 minutes. Oh yeah? Watch.

I would never suggest that you try this 15-minute roux as your first roux. The first time you go skiing, you don't go down the black diamond; you go down the bunny slope. The standard 45-minute method at left is safer and more traditional. But if you've made a roux before, give this a shot. This shit is intense, but it will save you a good half hour of cooking. You can substitute this method anywhere this book calls for a dark or caramel-colored roux. | *Makes 6 tablespoons*

¼ cup grapeseed oil   ¼ cup all-purpose flour

› Heat the oil in a Dutch oven over high heat until it just starts to smoke. You really need a Dutch oven for this, not a heavy skillet, because you need its extra depth to protect yourself from the hot oil. And don't forget that long-handled spoon.

› When the first little whiffs of smoke start to rise from the oil, dump in your flour and immediately start stirring. Stir like you mean it. Do not walk away. Do not answer the phone. It's really gonna go. Just stir, scraping the bottom and edges well to keep the flour from burning. It should be the right color in about 15 minutes. As with a traditional dark roux, add your trinity the moment your roux hits the color you want.

INSTANT ROUX

I used to think instant roux was evil, but I've come around. If you don't have a lot of culinary experience, just don't have time, or the thought of spending 45 minutes cooking roux—or my 15-minute roux inferno—scares the hell out of you, instant roux is not a bad idea. I even keep some at home. If you're making just a little batch of peas or if you want to thicken up your sauce or a stew real quick, instant roux is a wonderful little get-out.

Now, I've NEVER used instant roux in gumbo. But if you had to, in a pinch, well, I guess it'd work out alright. On the back of the jar, there's usually even a recipe for gumbo. I wouldn't take it to a competition, and I wouldn't sell it at a restaurant, but I bet it makes the sort of gumbo where you'd be like, "I could eat this and watch *Game of Thrones.* Yeah, this is good."

HOMEMADE STOCK

H omemade stock is always going to be better than store-bought. It will have more collagen (which means more body) and a richer flavor, and you can adjust it to your taste. That being said, I won't hate you if you use store-bought. I realize most home cooks do. Just be sure to buy a low-sodium variety.

CROCK-POT CHICKEN STOCK

Making chicken stock with a slow cooker (Crock-Pot) is the easiest method I've come across. Whenever I have something I need to cook low and slow overnight, my Crock-Pot is the way to go. It's got safety features already built into it—you couldn't bring it to a hard boil if you wanted to—and since it's insulated and covered, you don't have to worry about losing much liquid to evaporation. I can't be the only one that does this. It just makes so much sense. So give it a shot. Most people say to cook stock for 8 hours. But I've found 12 hours to be the sweet spot. | *Makes 10 cups*

1 roasted chicken carcass (meat removed)

1 whole chicken (remove the liver from any giblets)

1 large onion, peeled and quartered

1 large carrot, peeled and roughly chopped

2 ribs celery, roughly chopped

5 bay leaves

1 cup dry white wine

1 bunch fresh parsley, stems and all

2 tablespoons toasted whole black peppercorns

12 cups cold water

EQUIPMENT
4.5-quart (or larger) slow cooker

Note: If you don't have a slow cooker, you can make the stock in a large 10-quart stockpot and let it simmer uncovered all day on your stove's lowest setting. With the stovetop method, there is a greater chance that it could boil over, so even though all of this fits in a 4.5-quart slow cooker, you'll need the larger stockpot for the stove.

› Put everything in the slow cooker and cover with the lid. Crank it to high. As soon as it comes to a simmer, turn down to the lowest setting and cook for 12 hours.

› Carefully strain the liquid through a fine mesh colander or cheesecloth. Save the meat from the whole chicken for gumbo. The carcass and veggies go in the trash.

› The stock is ready to use immediately, refrigerate for a few days, or freeze for up to 3 months.

› If you aren't planning to use the stock in a few days, bring it to a boil in a stockpot over high heat and boil until reduced by three-quarters to 2½ cups, about one hour. Let cool, then freeze the concentrated stock in ice cube trays. This gives you little pockets of stock that you can reconstitute with water (6 tablespoons of water to one 2-tablespoon stock cube). Sometimes I even use the concentrate straight; it makes the best, richest gumbo.

CROCK-POT DUCK AND VEAL STOCKS

For wild game dishes, I like to use **duck stock.** It amps up the flavor in those dishes and gives you something to do with bird carcasses once you've eaten all that glorious meat. I use **veal stock** anytime I braise meats, make short ribs, or cook sides for meat dishes, like the barley for my venison (page 220). To make either stock, use the same method as making chicken stock, but with two roasted duck carcasses or 6 pounds roasted veal knuckle bones instead of the chicken carcass and whole chicken.

TO ROAST DUCK BONES

2 roasted duck carcasses (meat removed)

2 teaspoons kosher salt

2 teaspoons grapeseed oil

› Preheat the oven to 400°F. Season each duck carcass with 1 teaspoon salt and rub with 1 teaspoon oil. Place in a roasting pan and roast for 20 minutes, until the bones are nicely browned and have a little char on them.

TO ROAST VEAL KNUCKLE BONES

6 pounds veal knuckle bones (you can also use oxtails or beef spareribs)

1 teaspoon grapeseed oil

½ teaspoon kosher salt

1 cup full-bodied red wine (like cabernet)

› Preheat the oven to 400°F. Rub the bones with the oil and salt and place in a large roasting pan. Roast for 20 minutes, until the bones are nicely browned with a little char. Set the bones aside. While the pan is hot, deglaze with the red wine, scraping the bottom of the pan with a wooden spoon to release the browned bits. Add the wine and deglazed bits into the slow cooker with the bones and other ingredients.

CRAWFISH STOCK

This recipe uses crawfish, but it also works with lobster, crab, or shrimp. I like to use it wherever you might use fish stock, but want a little more intense flavor. I especially love to use it in Crawfish Bisque (page 86) and Crawfish Cornbread Dressing (page 88).

Now, I've never bought crawfish just to make stock. My crawfish for stock are always whatever is left over from a backyard crawfish boil (page 72). If you're smart, every boil ends with a crawfish peeling party, where your drunk friends stand around and finish peeling whatever crawfish are left on the table, saving all those heads and casings. If you're dumb, you're doing it yourself.

Typically at the end of a boil you'll be too drunk or tired to actually make stock, so throw the peeled heads, shells, and tail meat in the fridge to work on the next day. You can also freeze the parts if you can't get to it immediately. | *Makes 10 cups*

10 pounds boiled crawfish, chilled

1 cup brandy

20 cups water

1 large onion, peeled and quartered

2 ribs celery, roughly chopped

1 large carrot, peeled and roughly chopped

10 cloves garlic, peeled and crushed with the back of a knife

5 bay leaves

› Peel and devein the boiled crawfish, separating and reserving the heads, shells, and tail meat. Put the tail meat aside for another recipe, like Crawfish Bisque (page 86)—it's too delicious to become stock. If your crawfish were boiled with spices, as in a crawfish boil, use very cold water to give the crawfish heads and shells a rinse and remove all the spice and excess salt. For the record, my mom doesn't do this rinsing step, which makes for a salty stock—which is fine.

› Put the brandy in a small saucepan over high heat, then carefully ignite it with a long-handled lighter. Allow the flame to burn out on its own and reduce the brandy to ½ cup.

› In a 3-gallon pot, add the reduced brandy, cold water, all the crawfish heads and shells (about a gallon's worth), and the rest of ingredients. Take a mallet, potato masher, or a stiff whisk and crush the shells in the pot. Don't be shy. It helps get the flavor out of the heads.

› Crank the heat to high and bring the liquid in the pot up to a hard boil. Reduce heat to medium and keep at a low boil, uncovered, for 3 hours. Afterward, strain the stock through a fine mesh colander to remove the shells. But don't skim it. All that fat and protein on top helps give this stock its super-concentrated crawfish flavor.

EASY SEAFOOD STOCK

When my dad makes seafood stews (like Dr. Brent Toups' Seafood Gumbo, page 170), he's got his own stock preferences. Basically he takes whatever scrap vegetables and seafood carcasses or shells he's got on hand from previous meals (he fills a large ziplock in the freezer until he's got enough to use) and puts them in a stockpot, and adds enough water to the pot to cover it all. Then he cranks it up on high and boils it for about an hour. He then strains the stock in a fine mesh colander or cheesecloth and he's good to go.

Pepper Paste of Pain

Chicken Stock

Dark Roux

Creole Mustard

Creole Mustard Aioli

Cajur

Crack Spice

Cane Vinegar Aioli

BASICS

EVERYDAY RICE

Rice is central to Cajun culture. We're prideful about it because we grow it. Cajuns cooked local before it was cool to go local. Rice, sugarcane, crawfish—why do we eat that? Because we grow it and it's goddamn delicious. | *6 cups (serves 6 to 8)*

3 cups Louisiana jasmine rice (or any medium-grain white rice)

6 cups water

2 teaspoons kosher salt

2 bay leaves

Note: If you're using the rice for something else, like Dirty Rice (page 96), spread it out in a single layer on a baking sheet and refrigerate immediately.

› Put everything in a 4-quart saucepan over medium-high heat and bring to a boil. Reduce the heat and bring to a bare simmer. Stir, cover, and simmer for 10 minutes.

Remove from the heat and let steam in the covered pan for another 10 minutes, until all water is absorbed. Fluff with fork. Serve or cool immediately.

CREOLE MUSTARD

In the rest of the country, most people grow up with French's yellow mustard and Grey Poupon. I grew up with Zatarain's Creole mustard. It's not as intense as real Dijon, but it's richer than French's. My version has more of that Dijon intensity and is especially good with charcuterie, on a cheese board, and in a roast beef sandwich. You should make it the day before you want to use it. | *Makes 2½ cups*

1 cup whole yellow mustard seeds

1 cup cider vinegar

1 cup honey

1 teaspoon kosher salt

› Pour the mustard seeds into a blender and grind for 10 seconds, until the seeds are a fine powder. (If you don't have a high-powered blender, grind the seeds in a spice grinder first and then transfer to your blender.)

› Add the vinegar, honey, and salt to the blender and blend on medium for 10 seconds. With a spoon or spatula, scrape down the sides. Crank the blender up

to its highest speed and go for about 30 seconds. It will be a little soupy. Put in a food-safe container with a lid and let sit overnight to thicken. Since you're working with the mustard in powder form, it will absorb some of the liquid over time and get to the consistency you expect of mustard. The mustard will keep, refrigerated, almost indefinitely.

CREOLE MUSTARD VINAIGRETTE

This is my go-to dressing for butter lettuce or mixed greens salad. It's also one of the best dipping sauces of all time—use it on fried frog legs (page 224), with sausage (page 40), or with Hog's Head Cheese (page 38). | *Makes 2½ cups*

¼ cup cane syrup

¼ cup Creole Mustard (page 17), or store-bought

½ cup cane vinegar or cider vinegar

½ tablespoon fresh thyme leaves, finely chopped

½ teaspoon kosher salt

½ teaspoon black pepper

1½ cups neutral vegetable oil, like canola or grapeseed

› Put the cane syrup, mustard, vinegar, thyme, salt, and pepper in a blender and pulse for 10 seconds, or until it is all mixed together. With the blender on medium, drizzle in the oil until all of the oil is well incorporated. The vinaigrette will keep tightly covered in the refrigerator for up to 2 weeks.

CRACK SPICE

This is my version of a Cajun all-purpose seasoning. You have to use popcorn salt, because even iodized table salt won't stick to fried foods the way popcorn salt will. Use it on my cracklins (page 32), on popcorn, and anytime a recipe calls for Cajun or Creole seasoning. The addition of the sugar allows you to add a lot of ground chile without adding heat—sugar cancels out capsaicin. Store in an airtight container. | *Makes 1 cup*

6 tablespoons popcorn salt

6 tablespoons ground chile de arbol (or 3 tablespoons each cayenne pepper and smoked paprika)

3 tablespoons ground white pepper

3 tablespoons granulated garlic

3 tablespoons celery salt

3 tablespoons sugar

› Combine all the ingredients in a large bowl. Stir gently with a whisk to combine. And cover your mouth and nose while you do this. Trust me.

ISAAC'S CAJUN BOIL SPICE

When I'm boiling crawfish, this is the spice mix I use. You can substitute with something like Zatarain's Pro Boil—but then why'd you buy my book? This blend is better, plus making it can clear out a head cold. You'll have enough for one boil plus a little extra. Keep it around: The shelf life, stored in an airtight container, is basically infinite. | *Makes just over 7 cups*

2 cups popcorn salt

1 cup mustard powder

1 cup ground white pepper

1 cup celery salt

1 cup granulated garlic

1 cup sugar

½ cup cayenne pepper

› Like you do for the Crack Spice, cover your mouth and nose with a handkerchief while you put this together.

Combine all the ingredients in a large bowl. Stir gently with a whisk to combine.

ISAAC'S MAYONNAISE

I'm big on mayonnaise. My wife, Amanda, jokes all the time that our next restaurant should have an aioli tasting menu because I can work mayonnaise or aioli into nearly anything. I love to double and triple down on flavors, so working spices from a dish into a mayo is second nature to me.

Homemade mayo is always better, so do it that way if you can—and try to use farm-fresh eggs, because they taste better. But if I'm just picking some mayo up from the store, my favorite is Blue Plate. It's thick, it's tangy, and it's Louisiana-made. If you prefer another brand, I won't hate on you. But if you just don't like mayonnaise at all, we probably won't ever be real friends. | *Makes about 2 cups*

4 egg yolks

2 tablespoons Dijon mustard

2 tablespoons white wine vinegar

2 teaspoons kosher salt

2 cups neutral vegetable oil, like canola

› In a food processor, combine the egg yolks, mustard, wine vinegar, and salt. Pulse several times until all ingredients are mixed together. With the motor running, very slowly drizzle in the first ½ cup of oil; once the oil has emulsified, you can pour in the rest. The whole process should take about 30 seconds. A lot of people go too slowly when making mayo, and the oil warms up and the mayo can break on you. Some cooks do this in a mixer with a whisk attachment, but I think that adds too much air. I like a thick mayo, not a light fluffy mayo.

› Keep refrigerated and use within 4 days.

ESPRESSO MAYONNAISE

This mayonnaise is like making a coffee vinegar—it's super concentrated. It's good slathered on country ham (especially as part of a ham and mustard sandwich), on fried pork chops, as a dip for cracklins (page 32), or just to keep on hand at the hunt camp.

› Make Isaac's Mayonnaise, but substitute apple cider vinegar for the white wine vinegar and add 2 tablespoons espresso powder and 2 tablespoons brown sugar before you add the oil.

CANE VINEGAR AIOLI

This is the marriage of my vinegar and aioli obsessions. It's like my two fetishes got together and did the nasty. It's a great dipping sauce for anything that's fried, and has the fat and acid to complement fried shrimp, oysters, and frog legs. I use it in lieu of spritzing fish and chips with malt vinegar. Cane vinegar is made from fermented sugarcane juice—sugarcane grows all over south Louisiana.

› Make Isaac's Mayonnaise, but substitute ¼ cup cane vinegar for the white wine vinegar.

CREOLE MUSTARD AIOLI

When you want a mayo with an intense mustard flavor to complement rich meats, go for this. It's like Dijonnaise cranked up to eleven.

› Make Isaac's Mayonnaise, but add ½ cup Creole Mustard (page 17) or store-bought Creole mustard before you add the oil.

• CAJUN GAMES •

CADILLAC

Know blackjack? Well, Cadillac is a game of 31 instead of 21. And instead of keeping every card you pick up, you discard so that you always have 3 cards in your hand. It's a draw-and-discard game, where you try to get the card values—all cards must be in the same suit—to equal 31 (aces count as 11, face cards count as 10). If you're really close to 31, skip your turn and say "call." Everybody else gets one more turn and you throw down. The hand closest to 31 wins.

ISAAC'S PEPPER PASTE OF PAIN

The paste of pain is just pickled fresh peppers all whirred up, and I use it whenever I'd use hot sauce. The instructions are simple: Take some peppers, remove the stems (leave the seeds), and buzz them up in the food processor. Warm up white wine vinegar and pour it over. That's it. It's wonderful.

The paste has a bright fresh flavor and is the most versatile damn thing in the world: Throw a spoonful into everything from gumbo to scrambled eggs. Or, you can mix it with some ground pork and make a killer sausage (page 40). Anytime you want to use red pepper flakes or cayenne, use the paste instead. I like to make it with jalapeño or serrano peppers, but you can use any pepper you want. You can even use habaneros or Thai chiles, but watch the fuck out, Jack! | *Makes about 5 cups*

1 quart fresh jalapeño or serrano peppers, or your favorite local hot pepper

10 garlic cloves, peeled

1 quart white wine vinegar

1 teaspoon kosher salt

› Remove the stems from the peppers (leave the seeds). In a food processor, buzz all the peppers and garlic together until it looks like a relish.

› In a 4-quart saucepan over high heat, bring the vinegar and salt just to a boil.

› Put the pepper-garlic mixture in a large nonreactive heatproof mixing bowl, and pour the hot vinegar on top.

› Let cool to room temperature. It will keep in an airtight container in the fridge for up to 6 weeks. Shake it up before you serve it.

ISAAC'S WOODEN SPOONS

I'm always chopping wood. I chop wood for relaxation. I chop wood for my wood-burning oven (a couple of cinder blocks and a metal grate). In general, I like to build my own stuff and use my hands as much as I can. I'm not good at it, but I'm tenacious.

I was chopping some oak wood—good ole St. Charles Avenue oak—and I noticed there was a naturally forming divot in one of the planks. I thought: that would make a cool spoon. So I started cutting away, and after a couple of weeks picking it up and messing with it (probably about four hours of actual work), I carved out a spoon. I dropped the spoon in a hot fryer of peanut oil to cure, and it's now hard as a rock. You could beat someone to death with it. You know how some mamas smack you on the knuckles with a spoon when you're being a little shit? This one would break your hands. Every so often it frays, and I just burn off the ragged edges.

People ask me to make spoons for them, offer to pay me. Nope. If you have one of my spoons, it's a gift and I love you. That's something you can't buy.

THE BOUCHERIE

Boudreaux, Thibodeaux, and Fontenot are sittin' down at the fire. They drinkin' a little whiskey, they gettin' a little cocky. Boudreaux starts off, "One time, I was having sex with three women. And all three of their husbands showed up and I beat the piss out of each one."

Thibodeaux follows up. "One time, I went into a field, I beat up three bulls, three big Brahman bulls. I brought them down and beat the shit out of them, and then I fucked all their cows."

Fontenot, he don't say nothing. He just stirs the fire with his dick.

Boucheries were an essential part of life back in the day when a whole community would lend a hand in slaughtering, butchering, and cooking hogs or sheep. Refrigeration was scarce and you needed all hands on deck. They weren't for hoopin' and hollerin'.

They were as common as doing the washing on Sunday. But over the years, boucherie traditions died down. They just weren't necessary anymore. Now, people are getting back into the old ways of doing things, and they're making a comeback.

At a boucherie, you take an animal from "live to eating" in a few hours—that's the basic process. It's a wonderful exercise. You just have to shoot an animal in the head and then stick a knife in its throat and bleed him out.

It starts at daybreak. You're tired because you've been in the middle of a field camping and drinking all night. You get up. The pig, usually a Berkshire, is plump and has been very well taken care of. A prayer is said for the pig, and a thank-you is offered, acknowledging you couldn't do this without the pig giving its life. The slaughter is an homage to the animal—we're not into torture.

Killing the pig is quick and anti-climactic. It's not loud. It's not funny. You come up gently with a low-caliber pistol, a .22 or a .38. You use a full metal jacket and shoot him in the head. This way the heart keeps pumping blood. After you shoot him, you drag him over to the side of a trailer, put his head over a bucket, and puncture his jugular. You collect that blood while whisking in salt and vinegar to keep it from coagulating. Later on, you make Blood Boudin (page 30) with it.

After the pig is shot, a three-piece Cajun band starts playing somber, respectful music on a violin, guitar, and accordion. I always thought this was a nice touch and it almost makes me cry each time.

After you've drained the blood, the pig is dragged by several dudes—it's probably about 300 pounds—to a makeshift table of reinforced plywood set up on heavy-duty sawhorses. You've got huge crawfish pots full of water boiling. You dip big burlap oyster sacks into the boiling water and drape them across the pig and then pour more boiling water on top. This loosens the hair. A lot of it will come off in clumps just using your hands. Then you scrape the rest of the hair off, starting with a bell scraper and then a straight razor or a chef's knife. There's always little hairs that won't scrape off. For those, we use a butane tank with a straight shooter on it—a "Cajun flame thrower." It singes the rest of the hair off.

You're in it now. Turn the pig belly up and gut him. You start at the top, breaking the sternum with a knife. Crack it open, splay his chest out, and remove the guts—carefully. You save the lower intestines to rinse out for boudin. You save most of the organs to cook. There's only a small pile of things that aren't usable: gall bladder, sphincter, testicles. We've tried cooking them every which way, and they really do suck.

The steam rises off the animal in the early morning air. The gutting is something you'll remember for the rest of your life. If you've never smelled fresh guts from an animal…holy shit, it's visceral.

Next you take out his tenderloins from underneath the spine, and remove the head and hooves. The head gets cleaned to go into Hog's Head Cheese (page 38), the dish that takes the longest at the boucherie, so that gets started early. The hooves go to Trotters and White Beans (page 46). And then you start breaking the rest of the animal down, with the head butcher climbing on top of the pig on the plywood table. The shoulders go to boudin (page 28). The legs go to ham (page 52). The stomach, or ponce, goes to chaudin (page 56)—it will be stuffed and braised. The belly and any excess skin go to fried cracklins (page 32). The backbone and the rest of the big bones go to backbone stew (page 49).

At the boucherie, it's not uncommon to slaughter other animals. Lamb, goats, geese—we're already butchering, so it's kind of a "might as well" mentality. Plus, no matter how much you love pork, it can be nice to get a flavor break. With the lamb, it's a slightly more peaceful kill than with the pig. There's no gunshot. Instead, the butcher climbs into the crate with the lamb and pets and hugs it to calm it down. Then, swift as lightning, it's a knife to the throat.

Most of the time, boucheries happen in a big field littered with hay bales, with pickup trucks backed up into a semicircle. You're lucky if you have any proper facilities, like a sink. I've been to some where the only water supply is a 55-gallon drum someone hauled in his truck. And we don't do them when it's real hot, because that would be miserable. You're already going to sweat your ta-ta off.

BOUDIN
BALLS AND SAUSAGES

Boudin is a unique cajun sausage made from pork, rice, and liver. It is time-intensive, but not hard to make. If you can put a pork butt in the oven, you have all the skill you need. And the ingredients are easy to find: No matter where in the country you are, you can make great boudin.

Since we have a fresh sausage on the Meatery Board at the restaurant every day, I make fried boudin balls instead of stuffing the boudin into casings. But if you don't want to make balls or stuff in casings, you can throw some of the loose mixture in with scrambled eggs. Or pack it in a burrito. Or get a pistolette (a little individual French bread), poke a finger in it, stuff it with boudin, and deep-fry the whole thing. | *Makes 48 (2-ounce) boudin balls or 10 (8-ounce) links*

1 (3½-pound) bone-in pork shoulder (aka Boston butt)

3 tablespoons kosher salt, divided

2½ tablespoons black pepper, divided

1 large onion, roughly chopped

2 large ribs celery, roughly chopped

2 red bell peppers, roughly chopped (large chunks of about 1½ inches)

2 cups (about 100 cloves) of garlic (Yes, it's ridiculous. Buy it pre-peeled.)

4 cups amber beer

4 cups water

1 pound chicken livers

1 cup Louisiana jasmine rice (or any medium-grain white rice)

2 bunches green onions, tops only, chopped

1 tablespoon smoked paprika

1 teaspoon cayenne pepper (don't be a weenie)

FOR BOUDIN BALLS

4 cups unseasoned breadcrumbs

About 2 quarts peanut oil

Creole Mustard Aioli (page 19) and Squash Pickles (page 138), for serving

FOR BOUDIN SAUSAGE

12 feet of natural hog casings

Saltines or white bread, for serving

EQUIPMENT

Meat grinder (optional)

Note: A meat grinder is not necessary for boudin. You can shred the pork up with knives, forks, or by hand—that's more than good enough for home eating.

› Preheat the oven to 400°F.

› Score the pork shoulder: Make cuts 1 inch deep and 2 inches long on both sides, making a diamond pattern across the entire hunk of meat. Season with 2 tablespoons of the salt and 2 tablespoons of the black pepper. Aggressively rub it all over and in the scored crevices.

› Place the pork butt in a roasting pan that is deeper than the pork butt and will allow you to cover it. Roast, uncovered, for 40 minutes, turning it over halfway through. Remove from oven and reduce oven temperature to 325°F.

› Add the onion, celery, bell pepper, and garlic to the pan with the pork butt; they should go straight into the juices sitting in the bottom of the pan. Don't skim that fat off. It's counterintuitive to classic French cooking, but Cajuns leave all that good shit in there. Add the beer and water. Cover the pan with a lid or by tightly wrapping the top with aluminum foil.

› Put it back in the 325°F oven. Now we're braising the meat with the vegetables. Braise for 2½ to 3 hours, until the meat literally falls off the bone like pulled pork, then remove from the oven. Remove the meat from the braising liquid. Strain the braising liquid into a saucepan. Put the strained vegetables and aromatics back in the pan. Add the livers to the pan and put it back in the 325°F oven. Cook until the livers reach an internal temperature of 150°F, 10 to 12 minutes. Put the pork back in the pan with the veggies and livers.

› Meanwhile, place the rice in the braising liquid. Don't worry about measurements; any leftover liquid is going in the boudin. Over high heat, bring rice and braising liquid to a boil. Cover, reduce to a simmer, and cook for 10 minutes. Remove from heat and let rest 10 minutes.

› Break the pork butt into 2- to 3-inch chunks. You don't need to make it perfect because you're going to put it in the meat grinder. In the meat grinder, grind the pork butt with the veggies, cooked chicken livers, and any juice left in the roasting pan. If you don't have a meat grinder, you can do a Morimoto-style chop with two knives and cut the pork into a small coarse dice. You can put the veggies and livers in a food processor, but you'll want to separately fold in the hand-chopped meat. Don't put the meat in a food processor or you'll emulsify the fat.

› In a large bowl, combine the ground pork and veggie mixture with the rice (and any leftover cooking liquid) and the green onions. Add the smoked paprika, cayenne pepper, and remaining 1 tablespoon salt and ½ tablespoon black pepper. Mix all together and taste for seasoning. Add more salt if necessary. Want it hotter? Add some more cayenne. But do not think you can leave the cayenne out. Cayenne is not freaking optional.

TO MAKE BOUDIN BALLS

› Pack the boudin mixture into a container—Tupperware, the roasting pan, a bowl—and cover with plastic wrap, pressing the plastic against the surface of the meat. Place it in the fridge to chill completely, at least 3 hours but preferably overnight. You want the temperature of the boudin mixture to be 38°F (roughly the temperature of your fridge).

› Once chilled, scoop out the meat with an ice cream scoop into 2-ounce balls. (Or weigh them out—at the Meatery I literally weigh every single boudin ball that goes out of my kitchen. I'm psychotic like that.) Roll the boudin balls in the breadcrumbs. Really give them a good roll. Let the rolled balls rest in the fridge for 30 minutes.

› Meanwhile, heat about 5 inches peanut oil in a Dutch oven (or deep fryer) to 380°F. Place the boudin balls in the hot oil and fry for 3 to 4 minutes, until deeply browned and warmed all the way through. Do not agitate the balls while frying. They are full of water and will explode and you'll have a hot mess. The balls will sink in the oil when frying, so no need to even touch them.

› Remove the balls from the oil and place on paper towels or a wire rack to drain. Serve with Creole Aioli (page 19) and Squash Pickles (page 138).

TO MAKE TRADITIONAL BOUDIN SAUSAGES IN CASINGS

› Let the pork and rice mixture cool to room temperature. It will be loose and liquidy. Form into sausage links as per page 43. We stuff them pretty tight.

› Fill a large stockpot—at least 7 quarts—three-quarters full of water. Heat the water to 185°F, a very low simmer. Gently add the sausages and watch the pot carefully. If you go too hot on these, the casing will rip and the sausage will explode. Not like TNT, but you'll be sad. Cook in the simmering water for 10 to 12 minutes. The casings should be pretty taut, and if you cut one open, it should be steaming at the center.

› Serve immediately or freeze for up to 6 months. To serve immediately, slide the boudin out of the casings to eat on saltines or a slice of white bread. No mayo. No mustard. The white bread is basically your napkin and also keeps your hand from burning and getting greasy. The bread is strictly utilitarian.

› If you freeze them, when you're ready to serve, let the links defrost in the fridge. Rub them with a teaspoon of oil and roast in a 400°F oven for 15 to 20 minutes, flipping every 5 minutes. They'll burst a little bit. That's okay here; you'll also get a delicious crispy casing.

Boudin Balls

Blood Boudin

BLOOD BOUDIN

Follow the same recipe as boudin (previous page), but add 1 cup pork blood at the same time that you add the rice and green onions, after it is all ground and mixed and still warm. This only works if you're going to take the time to pipe it into casings. You can't do blood boudin balls because they've got too much moisture. We definitely do this at the boucherie, when we've got ample pig's blood on hand.

Boudin Sausages

CRACKLINS
(GRATTONS)

Cracklins, also called *grattons,* are deep-fried chunks of pork belly and skin. But they're so much more than that. If I could only eat one Cajun food for the rest of my life, it would be cracklins. They are the most unique dish that comes from Cajun culture, and they make me insanely happy. At a boucherie, cracklins are often the first things ready to eat. Once you holler "grattons!" everyone comes running.

Sit back, relax, and read this recipe all the way through, because cracklins rely strictly on technique. This is one of the trickiest recipes in this book. My boudin (page 28), which has about 20 ingredients and just as many steps, is easier to master. But don't worry if your cracklins don't come out perfect. Even a bad cracklin is still pretty damn good. And don't get too sure of yourself if your first batch *does* come out right. Perfection boils down to one minute in either direction. | *Makes about 6 cups (1 pound)*

2 pounds skin-on pork belly	1 gallon peanut oil	**EQUIPMENT**
3 cups lard	Crack Spice (page 18)	2 (13-quart) Dutch ovens

Note: If you can't get skin-on pork belly, you can't make this. But if you only have the skin, without much meat or fat attached, that's fine. I use the leftover lard I have from previous batches of doing cracklins, but you can use store-bought.

› Cut the pork belly into chunks, each with a square of skin about 1¼ inches wide. The height of the cracklin doesn't matter. Some might be nothing but skin, and others might have 2 inches of meat attached. Throw in odd ends, even the nipples—those end pieces become ultra seasoned, like the crumbs at the bottom of a chips bag, and can be the best part.

› Start with a cold 13-quart Dutch oven (at a boucherie, this would typically be done in a large cauldron). It should be large enough to hold the pork belly chunks and cover them in rendered lard by at least an inch.

› Add the cold lard and cold skin-on belly to the cold pot. Turn the heat to medium-high. As the lard starts to melt, give the pork belly a gentle toss with a wooden spoon, and make sure the pieces of pork belly are separated—they're naturally going to want to stick together. As the lard melts and the fat renders, the oil in the pot should be 240°F. That's the ideal temperature for rendering the cracklins.

› As the belly renders down, it's going to create more lard. Stir very gently; if you cause too much commotion the skin will separate from the meat and fat. It's not like a roux where you stir with reckless abandon. This is the hardest thing to learn: the technique of the first render. Just give the pieces of pork belly an occasional nudge so they don't stick to the bottom of the pan. If you see bits of skin exposed, turn them back upside down to submerge them in the oil.

› Pull the rendered cracklins off the heat when the skin starts to blister and the outsides are uniformly golden brown (this can take 45 minutes to an hour). Take the whole Dutch oven off the heat and let the rendered cracklins sit in the oil and rest until they have completely calmed down, meaning that the oil is no longer bubbling or popping, about 10 minutes. Remove the cracklins with a spider or slotted spoon, and put them in a metal colander or on a wire rack set in a sheet pan so they can drain. (Don't place them on paper towels—they'll stick.) You don't need them to be

completely free of fat, you just don't want them sitting in a pool of lard.

› Let the cracklins cool for about 20 minutes in the fridge. Then take your second cold Dutch oven (again, at a boucherie, this would typically be done in a large cauldron) and add enough peanut oil to cover the

cracklins in oil by at least an inch with enough room for you to stir them without sloshing oil over the sides.

› Set the Dutch oven over high heat and preheat the oil to 380°F. Deep-fry the cracklins for about a minute, until the skin has puffed. Remove from the oil and drain (again, don't use paper towels). While they're still hot, season liberally with Crack Spice.

THE BOUDIN DIVIDE

Once you cross the Atchafalaya Basin Bridge heading west from Baton Rouge, you start seeing boudin and cracklins immediately. It's worth pulling off at any roadside spot you can find for fresh fried boudin balls—stuffed with cheese or without—links of boudin, and bags of cracklins still hot from the fryer. My rule on road cracklins is you have to eat whichever one you grab out of the bag first. There's no digging around to get the fattiest or meatiest one. That's cheating, you sorry bastard.

Some of my favorite spots are the Best Stop Supermarket, Don's Specialty Meats, and Billy's Boudin & Cracklins, all within two miles of each other in Scott, Louisiana. Once you get past Jennings, you're out of the prime territory. And pretty much anything north of I-10 isn't Cajun, it's just redneck.

RILLONS

This is the closest thing to meat candy I've ever eaten—basically a red wine–caramel pork belly. I've tried making rillons with whiskey, white wine, and Pernod. Red wine is still the best. We sometimes use excess caramel from these rillons in dessert at our restaurants, like a rillons fudge sauce. I like it when even our desserts have pork in them. | *Serves 8 to 10*

1 cup full-bodied red wine, like Malbec

1 cup sugar

1 pound pork belly, skin removed, cut into 1-inch cubes

½ tablespoon fresh thyme leaves, coarsely chopped

1 teaspoon kosher salt

½ teaspoon ground black pepper

› Preheat the oven to 400°F.

› In a medium pot, about a 4-quart capacity, combine the wine and sugar and bring to a boil over high heat, then reduce to a simmer. Cook until the liquid is reduced to 1 cup, about 10 to 15 minutes. You're basically making a syrup of red wine and sugar.

› Place the pork belly cubes in a roasting pan large enough for them to fit in a single layer. Sprinkle the thyme, salt, and pepper over the pork belly. Pour the red wine reduction over the pork. Give it a stir to make sure the pork cubes are evenly coated.

› Put in the 400°F oven. After 10 minutes, stir the rillons, making sure the pork belly cubes are fully coated and lacquered with the juice in the pan. Scrape down the sides well and return to the oven. After 5 more minutes, stir again. After this point, check the rillons every minute, giving them a good stir each time. A good

rillon is only a minute from burning. When in doubt, stir more frequently—that's how you prevent the caramel from burning. Keep baking them, stirring every minute, until you have a dark caramel. Depending on your oven, this can take 25 to 40 minutes total cooking time.

› When you pull the pan from the oven, give it one last good stir and bank the rillons at one end of the pan and angle the pan a little bit by putting a folded kitchen towel under that side to create a slope. The caramel will cool and stick, and the fat will slide to the bottom. Discard the fat.

› Once they're cool enough to eat, pop them in your mouth like they're crack rocks. Any caramel that's left over in the pan is a fantastic addition to any dessert. I like it over vanilla ice cream. Tell your friends it's bacon fudge sauce.

HOG'S HEAD CHEESE

This is real-deal Cajun food. It's a terrine made from the whole head of a pig—there's no dairy involved. Whole hog means head, too! Hog's head cheese is a great way to make use of every last scrap of meat and to preserve the meat for a tasty snack.

Hog's head cheese tucked into a slice of white bread is a snack I eat with one hand while I'm prepping in the kitchen. Or, if you want to get real fancy about it, put it on saltines or Ritz crackers, and garnish with pickled jalapeños and Creole mustard. | *Makes 64 (1-ounce) slices*

20 cloves garlic, peeled

10 sprigs fresh thyme

10 sprigs fresh oregano

1 cup black peppercorns

1 (20-pound) pig's head, with jowls, ears, eyes, tongue, and snout intact

3 onions, peeled and quartered

2 carrots, peeled and roughly chopped

5 ribs celery, roughly chopped

3 gallons (or more) water, enough to submerge the head

1 gallon amber beer (128 ounces, almost a 12-pack)

½ teaspoon curing salt (optional)

2 tablespoons juice from Pickled Jalapeños (page 139) or hot sauce

1¼ cups Isaac's Pepper Paste of Pain (page 21)

⅓ cup kosher salt

¼ cup black pepper, finely ground

½ teaspoon cayenne pepper

Pickled jalapeños, for serving (optional)

Creole Mustard (page 17 or store-bought), for serving (optional)

EQUIPMENT

Cheesecloth

Butcher twine

Note: If a little shoulder meat is attached to the pig's head, all the better. But at a minimum you need the whole damn head. Call around local butcher shops to find out who works with whole animals. They're the ones who will typically have a pig's head. If you don't have curing salt, don't worry. You're not actually preserving this, but the curing salt keeps the head cheese from oxidizing and changing color from pink to gray.

› Make a bouquet garni: put the garlic cloves, thyme, oregano, and peppercorns on a square of cheesecloth and tie it into a sack with butcher's twine.

› Place the bouquet garni, pig's head, onions, carrots, celery, water, beer, and curing salt (if using) in a large stockpot (large enough to hold the head). Bring to a boil, then reduce to simmer and cook uncovered for 8 hours. Remove the head, vegetables, and bouquet garni. Set the head aside and discard the vegetables and bouquet garni. Skim the fat from the liquid and reserve it. (Be thorough, but don't stress if you miss some.) You've now got pork stock in the pot.

› Bring the stock back to a boil and reduce to 2 quarts. This will take a while.

› When the head is cool enough to handle, pick off all the fat, skin, and meat and set aside. But make sure you have *all* of it—all the parts that are squishy. Pull the tongue out of the mouth while it's still warm and peel off the membrane and discard—most of the time it peels off like a sticker in one nice piece. If it's cold it sticks.

› If you're bold, go ahead and chop into the head with a cleaver (I use a carbon steel Dexter-Russell 2-pound butcher cleaver; it's a beast) and scoop the brains out. They are nearly liquefied jelly at this point. The brains are a pain in the ass to get to, but if you're already doing this whole mess, you might as well.

› In a large bowl (large enough to accommodate 2 quarts stock and all the meat), tear up all the meat and brains

with your hands into rough ¾-inch pieces. (I like to keep it uneven and chunky, so when you slice the head cheese you can recognize a piece of tongue or a piece of ear in it.) Add the reduced stock back to the meat. Add the jalapeño juice (or your favorite hot sauce), pepper paste, kosher salt, ground black pepper, and cayenne pepper. Mix with your hands until the mixture is homogenized; the liquid will keep trying to separate from the fat.

› Taste this for seasoning and adjust as necessary. At room temperature, it should taste a little oversalted and a little too hot and spicy. When you eat it cold, the spice level will be muted.

› When it's all mixed together you can chill it to firm it up, then slice it cold, or leave it spreadable at room temperature.

› Put it in pâté molds or ungreased casserole pans (like a 9 x 13-inch Pyrex baking dish; don't go out and buy something new). Fill the containers up to the top. Cover them with plastic wrap, pressing the plastic against the meat mixture. Refrigerate for at least 4 hours, or until the terrine has set and completely chilled through—it will be gelatinized.

› Remove from container. It should dump out easily, but you might have to run a butter knife around the edges. Cut into 2 x 2-inch blocks. Slice a block into ¼-inch slices and serve with pickled jalapeños and Creole mustard. If you've gone to the trouble of making hogshead cheese, I forgive you for using store-bought mustard.

› Serve to your friends. Tell them it's cheese. Laugh.

SAUSAGES

These are fresh sausages—I don't cure any of my sausages—but I do like to let the sausage air-dry for 2 hours after it's piped to dry up the casing some. That gives you the snap you want when you bite it.

The key to making sausage is keeping your ingredients really cold at all times when grinding. If you grind warm meat, it will get smeared instead of cut. You don't want that. If you don't have a grinder, you can get a butcher to grind the meat for you—and often even stuff it into casings— usually for a polite tip. I've had decent luck grinding the meat in a food processor, but honestly, it just doesn't come out the same.

CHICKEN, BACON, AND CILANTRO SAUSAGE

Yes, this recipe calls for a lot of garlic. One trick to making good sausage: Add more garlic. If you don't want to stuff the sausage into casings, you can form the meat into patties—this makes a killer chicken burger—or even a meatloaf. | *Makes 9 or 10 (5-inch) sausages*

- 3 pounds skinless boneless chicken legs and thighs
- 1 pound smoked bacon
- 1 cup packed cilantro (about 1 bunch), finely chopped
- ⅓ cup minced garlic (about 22 cloves)

- 1 tablespoon kosher salt
- 1 teaspoon ground black pepper
- ⅓ cup wheat beer (I like Canebrake.)

Natural hog casings, about 6 feet's worth

EQUIPMENT
Meat grinder
Sausage stuffer

› Put the chicken legs and thighs in freezer for 30 minutes before grinding. You need them to get really cold—almost frozen—but still pliable. Put the chicken and bacon through a meat grinder set to medium. After grinding, put the meat back in the freezer for 30 minutes to get it cold again.

In a large nonreactive bowl, add the chilled ground chicken and bacon, cilantro, garlic, salt, pepper, and beer. Mix and fold by hand for about a minute to emulsify the beer liquid with the fat. Work quickly, so it doesn't heat up again. When properly mixed, the meat mixture will have some spring to it—it will feel like a medium-rare steak to the touch—and have some chunks of fat still visible.

› Follow the *Make the Sausage* method, on the next page.

PEPPER PASTE OF PAIN PORK SAUSAGE

My favorite sausages have an intense flavor that comes from just three or four ingredients. This hot garlic sausage is one of my all-time personal favorites. It's simple, spicy, garlicky—a perfect "my first badass homemade sausage."

Always double down on flavor. For me, intensity is everything. If you put it in there, really put it in there. If I want the flavor of licorice in a dish, I'll put in Herbsaint and fennel seed and star anise. This sausage doubles down on the garlic because you've got it in the Pepper Paste of Pain and in the sausage itself. | *Makes 9 or 10 (5-inch) sausages*

3 pounds boneless pork butt

⅓ cup minced garlic (about 22 cloves)

¼ cup Isaac's Pepper Paste of Pain (page 21), or to your taste; I like it quite hot

2 tablespoons kosher salt

1 tablespoon ground black pepper

⅛ teaspoon curing salt (optional)

⅓ cup dark beer, like stout

Natural hog casings, about 6 feet's worth

EQUIPMENT

Meat grinder

Sausage stuffer

Note: Once you've combined the ground meats and seasonings, it's best to chill the mixture overnight before you form the sausages.

› Put the pork butt in freezer for 30 minutes before grinding. You want to get it really cold—almost frozen—but still pliable. Put the pork through a meat grinder set to medium. After grinding, put the meat back in the freezer for 30 minutes to get it cold again.

› In a large nonreactive bowl, combine the chilled ground pork, garlic, pepper paste, kosher salt, pepper, curing salt, and beer. Mix and fold by hand for about a minute to emulsify the beer liquid with the fat. Work quickly, so it doesn't heat up again. When properly mixed, the meat mixture will have some spring to it—it will feel like a medium-rare steak to the touch—and have some chunks of fat still visible.

› See *Make the Sausage* method.

MAKE THE SAUSAGE

› Cook and taste a sample of the sausage mixture (see "Taste Your Sausage," page 42) and adjust seasonings as needed.

› Wrap the bowl tightly with plastic wrap and put in the fridge for at least 1 hour (overnight is best). If your mixing bowl is too big for the fridge, transfer to a baking dish and wrap it tightly.

› When you're ready to stuff the sausage, rinse the hog casings by sticking one end directly on the faucet (like a water balloon) and running water through. Don't soak the casings or they'll get weak on you and end up busting. When they're well rinsed they should look clean and a little bit like a really long condom. (You wish.)

› Remove the meat from the fridge. Using the sausage stuffer, pipe and form the sausage mixture into links (see How to Stuff a Sausage, page 43).

› Put on a wire rack in the fridge to air-dry, uncovered, for 2 hours. This lets the sausage rest, but more importantly it lets the sausage casings dry.

› At this point you can freeze the linked sausage for up to 6 weeks to cook later. (When you thaw it, let it defrost in fridge; don't leave out at room temperature.) Or why wait? Fire that meat up to eat now!

› To cook: Preheat the oven to 300°F. Place the sausages on a wire baking rack set in a rimmed sheet pan and roast for about 15 minutes, until the internal temperature reaches 150°F. (The FDA says cook it to 165°F, but screw that. That's overcooked sausage.)

› Serve immediately. I like my sausages with Double Dill Pickles (page 147) or smeared with some grain mustard. And a white bread sausage sandwich is the shit. Tuck the link in some soft white bread with mustard and kill it.

TASTE YOUR SAUSAGE

It's important to taste your sausage meat (and terrines) before you go to the trouble of stuffing it into casings. Once the sausage is stuffed, it's too late to adjust the flavor. And you'd have done a lot of work for a wimpy piece of meat. To test: Preheat the oven to 300°F when you begin combining the ground meat and seasonings. Pinch off a little of the sausage mixture and bake in the oven on a baking sheet for about 6 minutes. Taste and adjust the seasonings.

HOW TO STUFF A SAUSAGE

Remove the meat from the fridge. Load your sausage mixture into a sausage stuffer. Tie off one end of the rinsed hog casings with a knot. Load onto the horn of the sausage stuffer, as if you are bunching a sock onto it. (It's better to have more casings than you think you'll need. For my recipes, you'll need about 5 feet, but go ahead and load 6 feet because you'll need some extra for twisting to make links and tie the ends.)

Once you have filled the casing with your sausage mixture, start with the tied end. At about 5 inches from the knot, lightly pinch and twist to form a single link. Skip ahead 5 inches and repeat. Continue until all of the sausage has been twisted into links. Once you reach the end, tie off the casing and cut off any excess.

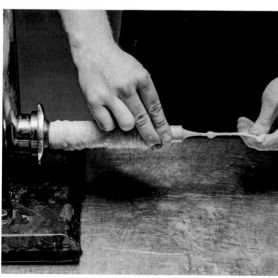

SAZERAC TERRINE

A terrine is a pâté that's cooked in a terrine mold. There's no quick get-out on a terrine: It needs to fully chill after it's been cooked, and it's best when prepared a couple of days in advance. The Sazerac is my favorite New Orleans cocktail. Invented here, it's made using good rye, Herbsaint, bitters, sugar, and orange. (I love those flavors so much that I turned my favorite drink into a meat dish. Of course.) For this one, we go to extremes to keep everything cold. Not only do you want your meat cold, but you also want the equipment to be as cold as possible. And I pack in the sweetness: orange, lemon, cherries. | *Makes 24 (1-ounce) slices*

1½ pounds ground pork butt, very cold

8 ounces ground pork belly, skin off, or fatback, very cold

¼ cup rye whiskey

¼ cup orange liqueur, like Grand Marnier or Triple Sec

2 tablespoons sugar

Grated zest and juice of 2 large navel oranges

Grated zest of 2 lemons (no juice)

½ cup Luxardo maraschino cherries (with syrup)

2 tablespoons nonfat dry milk powder

2 teaspoons fennel seeds, toasted and ground

¼ teaspoon *quatre épices* (French four spice: equal parts allspice, clove, cinnamon, and nutmeg)

1½ tablespoons kosher salt

⅛ teaspoon curing salt (optional, to preserve color and shelf life)

12 to 14 slices bacon

8 cups ice

Creole Mustard (page 17) or Dijon; pickled red onion; and Pickled Grilled Pineapple (page 142), for serving

EQUIPMENT

1 terrine mold (11½ x 3½ x 2 ½ inches)

Note: Be sure to get all the zest from the orange—but not the pith—because this is one of the main flavors of the terrine. And zest with a Microplane, not a bar zester, because you want the zest to be all broken up. A bar zester gives thick curls that don't blend well.

› Put the mixing bowl and paddle attachment of a large stand mixer, along with the ground pork butt and pork belly, in the freezer for 30 minutes.

› Combine the whiskey and liqueur in a small saucepan. Bring to a boil over high heat and reduce to 1 tablespoon, about 5 minutes. Be very careful: This may ignite. If it does catch on fire, just let the alcohol burn off. In the chilled bowl of the mixer, combine the reduced liqueur, sugar, orange zest and juice, and lemon zest. Give it a good whisk to dissolve the sugar. Chill until cold.

› Remove the meat from the freezer and add it to the mixture. Add the cherries (with juice), milk powder, fennel, four spice, kosher salt, and curing salt if using.

› Using the paddle attachment, combine the ingredients on medium speed for 15 seconds. Then crank it up to high and mix until the meat mixture starts to stick to the side of the bowl, about 30 seconds. The meat mixture should come together, but still be a little loose. All the juice and liquor should be incorporated; there should be no excess liquid at the bottom. Cook and taste a sample of the meat (see box page 42).

› Preheat the oven to 325°F. Drape the bacon slices into the terrine mold, lining them with about a ¼-inch overlap between slices and letting the excess bacon drape over the edges. Working with handfuls at a time, press the pork into the terrine mold, tamping down gently with the back of your forefinger and middle finger to remove air pockets. Wrap the excess ends of

the bacon over the top of the terrine to make a nice little package. Cover with lid and place the mold in a high-sided roasting pan. Add room temperature water to the roasting pan until it comes halfway up the side of the mold. Carefully place in oven and bake for 1 hour, until the terrine reaches an internal temperature of 150°F.

› Once it comes out of the oven, using an oven mitt, carefully remove the terrine mold from the roasting pan. Pour the hot water out of the pan. Place the terrine mold

back in the pan and add ice water until it reaches three-quarters of the way up the terrine mold. Refrigerate overnight.

› Turn the terrine out of the mold. Slice and serve with a little mustard, pickled red onion, and pickled pineapple.

TROTTERS AND WHITE BEANS

This is a bean dish flavored with pig. The trotters, or pig's feet, are full of collagen that gives up its stickiness to make a great pot of beans. We make it because as part of the boucherie you don't let anything go to waste. It's a way to take simple boiled beans and make them a meal really worth chowing down on. | *Serves 4*

- 4 pounds pig trotters (pig's feet), hooves off (if the trotters still have the shank attached, that's fine)
- 4 teaspoons kosher salt, divided
- 3 teaspoons finely ground black pepper, divided
- 2 tablespoons unsalted butter

- 1 medium onion, chopped
- 1 red bell pepper, chopped
- 2 ribs celery, chopped
- 10 cloves garlic, minced
- 1 pound dried white beans (Great Northerns or baby limas)
- 1 (12-ounce) bottle amber-style beer

- 5 cups pork or chicken stock (page 12, or low-sodium if using store-bought)
- 4 bay leaves
- 6 sprigs fresh thyme
- ½ teaspoon cayenne pepper
- Everyday Rice (page 17) and hot sauce or cider vinegar, for serving

› Preheat the oven to 400°F.

› Rub the trotters with 2 teaspoons salt and 2 teaspoons black pepper. Place the trotters on a baking sheet and roast, flipping halfway through, for 20 minutes. Set aside. Reduce the oven temperature to 350°F.

› Meanwhile, in a large Dutch oven over medium heat, melt butter and sweat the onion, bell pepper, and celery for 3 minutes. Add the garlic and sweat for an additional minute.

› Add the trotters, beans, beer, stock, bay leaves, thyme, cayenne, and remaining 2 teaspoons salt and 1 teaspoon pepper. When you add the trotters, be sure to add all drippings left on the pan. Cover the Dutch oven and

bake in the 350°F oven for 4 hours, until the trotters have broken up and become tender and the beans are fully cooked. Don't you dare skim the fat off the top. When it comes out of the oven, fold the fat right back into the beans. My proper French compatriots would frown on this, but the fat should be savored as part of the dish. Trotters aren't that fatty so you aren't getting a whole slick of oil on top. It's perfect.

› Serve the beans over white rice. Or even by itself. I sometimes serve the beans over my cornbread (page 134) with a little hot sauce garnish. My dad likes his beans over white bread. If you don't like hot sauce, spritz it with the same amount of cider vinegar.

HOG BACKBONE STEW

I'll start off by saying you can also do this with spareribs because I don't expect you to have easy access to a hog's backbone. This is the kind of thing you eat out of a bowl with a plastic spoon, standing up in a field—your basic pour-over-rice-and-eat-at-a-boucherie type of shit. Note that you're *not* going to be gnawing on a bone like a slab of ribs thinking, "Mmm, this meat is good." Instead, think of it like a damn fine Cajun rice and gravy. | *Serves 6 to 8*

4 pounds pork backbone (or bone-in rack of pork spareribs)

1 tablespoon kosher salt

2 teaspoons finely ground black pepper

6 tablespoons grapeseed oil, divided

¼ cup all-purpose flour

1 large onion, finely diced

1 red bell pepper, finely diced

2 ribs celery, finely diced

4 bay leaves

10 cloves garlic, minced

1 (12-ounce) bottle porter-style dark beer

¼ cup dark balsamic vinegar

4 cups water

¼ teaspoon cayenne pepper

Everyday Rice (page 17), for serving

› Season the bones with the salt and pepper. In a large Dutch oven, heat 2 tablespoons of the grapeseed oil over medium-high heat until it just starts to smoke. Sear the bones hard on all sides, 2 minutes per side. After all the meat is seared (will look like a browned steak that just came out of a broiler), set the bones aside on a plate. They're going to leach some juices and you want to save all of that. Don't remove the oil from the Dutch oven.

› In the Dutch oven over medium heat, make a dark roux (page 10), using the remaining 4 tablespoons grapeseed oil and the flour, about 45 minutes. Once the roux is the color of milk chocolate, add the onion, bell pepper, celery, and bay leaves and stir vigorously for 5 minutes to soften the vegetables and caramelize. Add the garlic and cook for an additional minute, stirring often. Add the beer and vinegar to deglaze and stir vigorously. Add

the water and bring to a simmer. (Don't bring to a boil and reduce to simmer; once I add roux to things I like to go slow so I don't burn the roux.) Stir continuously to emulsify the roux with your stock (water, beer, vinegar).

› Once it's simmering, add the bones and cayenne to the pot. Reduce the heat to medium-low, cover, and simmer for 3 hours. Any meat left on the bones will be completely cooked off and broken down and incorporated into the gravy—that's intentional. This is all about the gravy. You're never gonna get a lot of meat on the backbone anyway, unless you have a shitty butcher.

› Serve over rice in a Dixie bowl. I fucking love it.

TOMAHAWK THROWING

I love going medieval on shit, so hurling tomahawks at a giant wooden target just gets me tingly in all my bits. Think about it like pitching a baseball: You throw it hard and straight, with your arm going up and down, rotating your hips, and keeping your arm like an arrow on the follow-through. If your hand isn't pointing straight at the board after you release, you fucked up. When you throw it at an angle, the blade won't stick in the wood. Don't worry about flipping it. I promise, you will try to spin it exactly once, and it will scare the piss out of you. Just let momentum and gravity do the work for you. When you pull it out of the board, work it straight up and down. It's not a bottle cap, don't twist it. For my friend Kyle's 26th birthday, I showed up at 9 a.m. with the board, some tomahawks, and a six-pack of tall boys. I was like, "Happy birthday, I've got to go to work soon, so let's get started."

BOUCHERIE HAM

Boucherie ham is a raw ham, meaning it is not cured. At a boucherie it would be injected with a brine that's seasoned with an overt amount of garlic powder. I prefer fresh garlic. By using fresh garlic to make the brine, you also end up with a garlic paste to use to form a crust on the outside of the ham. At a boucherie, you'd probably cook this on a smoker or in a Cajun microwave (see page 91). This at-home version lets you use your oven instead. | *Serves 20*

1 (15-pound) raw ham, with skin, shank, hock, and aitch bone (hip bone) removed

2 cups (100 cloves) garlic, peeled

1 (12-ounce) bottle fruit-forward beer (I use an apricot hefeweizen)

1 cup cane syrup (or honey)

¼ cup apple cider vinegar

3 tablespoons plus 4 teaspoons kosher salt

1 tablespoon plus 2 teaspoons ground black pepper, divided

½ teaspoon cayenne pepper

EQUIPMENT

Large deep roasting pan

1 (1½-ounce) marinade injector

1 rolling pin, small baseball bat, or other implement of destruction

Note: The ham should still have the femur. The hip bone might still be connected. You can have your butcher remove the hip bone, or you can use a knife and brute force to rip it off. I'd say just ask your butcher to do it.

› Preheat the oven to 350°F.

› Wrap the ham in plastic wrap. Give it 9 or 10 good whacks with the rolling pin. Turn it and give 9 or 10 more good whacks. Flip it and give 9 or 10 more good whacks. Turn it and give 9 or 10 more good whacks. Beat the shit out of it. Seriously. *Tender-iiiiiize.*

› Put the garlic, beer, cane syrup, vinegar, the 3 tablespoons salt, 1 tablespoon black pepper, and cayenne pepper in a blender and blend on medium speed for 10 seconds. Strain the mixture by pouring it through a fine mesh colander or sieve into a bowl (or any other nonreactive food-safe container). Once this mixture is strained, you'll have your brine and a paste of garlic and spices left over—don't you dare throw that away. Pour the brine into something tall and cylindrical, like a drinking glass. (You're going to be filling an injector with the liquid, so having something tall and cylindrical just makes it easier to fill the injector.)

› Fill the injector with the brine, and start with the ham fat side up. In the top left corner of the ham, about 1½ inches from the edge, press the injector about halfway through the ham and inject ½ ounce (about 1 tablespoon) brine. Continue doing this, moving the injector 1½ inches over and repeating, then 1½ inches over and repeating, refilling the injector as necessary. You're going to make a grid on the ham every 1½ inches (across and up and down) until you have covered the fat side with a square grid of holes. Then turn the ham over and repeat. Some of the liquid will leak out, and that's okay. Once the top and bottom are injected, inject along the 4 sides at equal intervals. If you're being smart about this, you'll do it in the pan you're going to cook it in, so the juice stays contained and doesn't run all over your countertop.

› Place the ham in a large roasting pan, big enough to hold the ham. Season the top with 2 teaspoons salt and 1 teaspoon black pepper. Turn the ham over and season the bottom with the remaining 2 teaspoons salt and remaining 1 teaspoon black pepper. Take the reserved garlic mash and evenly distribute it across the surface of the whole ham. It won't spread very well, so press it and sort of pack it on.

› Place the ham fat side up and bake in the 350°F oven. After 1½ hours, pour 2 quarts warm water (just hot water out of your faucet) into the pan—not over the ham—and cover it with foil. Put it back in the oven and bake for 2 more hours, until the internal temp is 150°F (about 4 hours total cook time).

› Once it reaches that internal temp, pull it out of the oven, uncover, remove the ham from pan, and let rest for 20 minutes. Skim the fat from the jus in the roasting pan and discard; reserve jus. Then slice the ham, perpendicular to the bone, into ¼-inch slices, though thinner than that is better. The best knife to use is a scalloped serrated knife. The pointed ones will just tear the meat off; and because it's so crusty, a normal slicer isn't going to slice into the meat. A scalloped serrated knife will give you better control and nicer slices of ham. Although my dad would just use his electric knife—he loves any excuse to bust that fucker out. Pour reserved jus over slices of ham before serving.

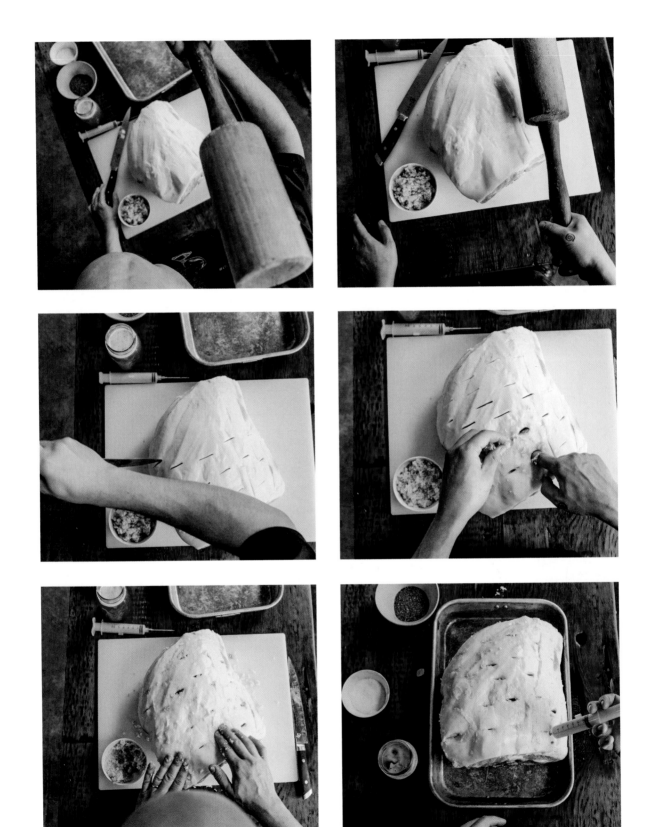

• CAJUN GAMES •

STUMP

You get a log that's about waist high. Everybody has a hammer, and everybody has a nail. You all tap your nails into the stump to the same height. The object of the game is to have your nail standing last. You take your hammer and flip it forward. Catch it. And try to strike someone else's nail. All without pausing. Flip it, catch it, and strike. Everybody takes a turn while standing in a circle. I haven't seen anyone get hit in the head yet.

CHAUDIN
(PONCE)

The word *ponce* refers to the pig's stomach. *Chaudin* is the boucherie dish you cook with the ponce. Normally, you buy your ponce already stuffed and smoked. But at the boucherie, you're on your own. It's essentially Cajun haggis—except it's good. | *Serves 4 to 6*

- 1 pig stomach
- 1 pound pork shoulder, cut into 1-inch chunks
- 4 ounces pork liver, cut into 1-inch chunks (roughly ⅔ cup)
- ¼ cup uncooked white rice (I use Louisiana jasmine)
- 1 medium onion, finely diced
- 10 cloves garlic, minced

- 1 large bunch green onions (greens and whites), finely sliced
- 1 jalapeño, seeded and finely diced
- 1 tablespoon kosher salt
- 1 teaspoon ground black pepper
- ¼ cup grapeseed oil
- ¼ cup all-purpose flour

- 1 (12-ounce) bottle amber beer
- 2 cups chicken stock (page 12 or store-bought); or pork stock if you've got it; I mean, shit, you managed to get yourself a pig's stomach

EQUIPMENT
Butcher twine
Larding needle
Meat grinder

PREP THE STOMACH

› Step one: Get a pig's stomach. Congratulations, you got a pig's stomach. Holy shit. If you didn't do a whole boucherie, I don't know where the hell it came from. Good job, buddy!

› Slice it open with a sharp knife to produce a 4- to 5-inch slit. You've got to clean out all the stuff it's been eating, like Oreos. I don't know why we give a pig Oreos before we shoot it, but we do. If you're a pig eating Oreos, there's tough news ahead, son. You're about to get wasted.

› Once it's cleaned out, give the stomach a scald. To scald, bring a large pot of water to boil and give the stomach a 1-minute blanch in it (a quick dip to tighten it up), then scrape the insides to remove any leftover bits or discolored spots. There's a little liner in there that you want to scrape off because it's been touching bile and whatnot. If you somehow order this from a butcher, make them do all this.

MAKE THE PORK FILLING

› Place the pork shoulder and pork liver chunks in the freezer for 30 minutes. Then run the shoulder through a meat grinder set to medium setting. Run the liver

through the grinder as well. (If you buy your pork already ground, you'd just need to grind the pork liver at this point. And if you don't have a grinder, you can puree it in a food processor or chop it finely with a butcher knife.)

› Combine the ground pork, ground liver, rice, onion, garlic, green onions, jalapeño, salt, and black pepper. Mix well with your hand or a rubber spatula until completely combined. You don't want to overwork this—don't overheat it—mix it quick and mix it well, but don't get too excited.

› Pack the mixture tightly into the pig stomach (the ponce). If it doesn't all fit, it's no problem. The leftover stuffing will go in the gravy later. Once the stomach is stuffed, the 4- to 5-inch slit from cleaning it should be able to close skin-to-skin like a football—you don't want it overlapping or gaping. With the butcher twine and the larding needle, stitch up the stomach—repair the wound, if you will. It's going to look like a football stitch meets a hospital suture. You want it touching skin to skin, but not overlapping. Watch a video on suturing— I'm serious. My dad taught me how (he's a dentist), so I've adopted that same method for tying meats and organs up.

› Or you could use butcher twine without the needle and tie it up like you'd tie up a roast. You don't need it hermetically sealed. You just want it to stay all together and not fall apart while you're cooking it.

MAKE THE GRAVY AND COOK THE PONCE

› In a large Dutch oven over medium heat, make a dark roux (page 10) using the oil and flour, about 45 minutes. Once the roux is the color of milk chocolate, add the beer and stir well all along the bottom (essentially deglazing it). Once it starts to thicken up (it will happen pretty quickly), add the chicken (or pork) stock and any extra stuffing. Keeping heat at medium, bring the mixture up to a simmer. Once it's simmering, reduce the heat to low and keep the liquid at a low simmer.

› Place the sewn-up stomach in that gravy. Cover the Dutch oven and simmer over low for 3 hours. Every 30 minutes, remove the lid and give the stomach a nudge with a spoon (just enough to keep it from sticking to the bottom) and baste the stomach with the gravy; replace the lid. Repeat three times (for 1½ hours). Then remove the lid and flip the stomach; replace the lid and simmer for 1½ hours longer, repeating the nudging and basting process every 30 minutes. After it's cooked for 3 hours, the stomach has braised down and is fork-tender, and the inside is basically a pâté. It's going to have the texture of meatloaf—I guess it is kind of a Cajun version of that. This is meatloaf, if meatloaf had balls.

› After braising it for 3 hours (gravy should be nice and thick), turn off the heat. Remove the chaudin from pan (leaving the gravy in the pan). This is a good time to check seasoning on the gravy. You'll notice we didn't add salt to the gravy—that's because a lot of the flavor gets leached out of the stuffing through the stomach into the gravy.

› Let the chaudin sit for a couple of minutes, then remove the butcher twine (I use tongs and a knife to do it because once it's cool enough to handle, I think it's too cool to eat, personally). When you cut it open, it's like braised pâté. Slice it into 1-inch slices and pour about 2 tablespoons of gravy over each slice to basically give it a roux gravy lacquer.

FRISSEURS with BLACK-EYED PEAS and COLLARDS

I didn't grow up eating frisseurs and had the dish for the first time at a boucherie several years ago. Of course, I'd heard of it, but nearly every person has a different definition, although most folks agree it's a heart, liver, and kidney stew. Ironically, the first time I ever ate it, I was the one who cooked it, just kinda guessing my way around the pot. I honestly don't know if what I did was right, but I was told I did good by some drunk, haggard old-timers. You know how reliable they are. If you're a full-blood Cajun and are one of the lucky ones who grew up eating this shit, then I'm jealous. You may not recognize my frisseurs as the thing you grew up with. But that's okay. You may not recognize half the stuff in this book if you're that hard-line. | *Serves 6 to 8*

- 3 pounds pork offal (from one pig, it might be 1 heart, 1 liver, 2 kidneys), all cut to about a 1-inch dice
- 4 teaspoons kosher salt, divided
- 2 teaspoons ground black pepper, divided
- 3 tablespoons neutral vegetable oil, such as canola or grapeseed, divided

- 1 large onion, finely diced
- 1 large red bell pepper, finely diced
- 2 ribs celery, finely diced
- 10 cloves garlic, minced
- 1 (12-ounce) bottle dark beer (I use porter)
- 2 quarts (8 cups) chicken stock (page 12 or store-bought)
- ¼ teaspoon cayenne pepper

- 5 bay leaves
- 1 pound dried black-eyed peas (unsoaked)
- 1 bunch collard greens (about 1 pound), deveined and roughly hand torn

Everyday Rice (page 17), for serving

Note: If you don't have any offal, you could make this dish with chicken liver or chicken hearts and pork shoulder. You won't get that entrail flavor that I know you're craving—but it'll work.

› Season the offal with 2 teaspoons of the salt and 1 teaspoon of the black pepper and toss well together in a bowl to make sure all the meat is seasoned.

› In a large Dutch oven, heat 2 tablespoons of the grapeseed oil over high heat until it is smoking hot—I want it to actually smoke. As soon as it starts smoking, add the offal. You might need to do this in batches so you don't crowd the pan. Sear that hard for 4 minutes, giving it a stir every minute or so. You don't want to stir it too much or you won't get a hard sear. Remove the offal from the Dutch oven and set it aside in a bowl or on a plate. Reduce the heat to medium and return the Dutch oven to the burner.

› Add the remaining 1 tablespoon oil to the Dutch oven and let it heat up for a minute (until it shimmers—or sizzles when you flick drops of water in it). Add the onion, bell pepper, and celery and sweat for 3 minutes, stirring occasionally with a wooden spoon, being sure to scrape the bottom of the pot to pull up the fond (the bits of charred meat from browning the offal). This is basically beginning the deglazing process. Stir in the garlic and sweat for another minute, stirring once more during the minute. Add the beer and bring up to a simmer (to bleed off most of the alcohol). Then add the stock and remaining 2 teaspoons salt, remaining 1 teaspoon black pepper, the cayenne pepper, and bay leaves, and stir. Add the black-eyed peas, collard greens, and finally the browned offal (be sure and put the

collards in before the meat so the weight will mash the greens down and help fit everything in the pot). Crank the heat up to high and bring the liquid to a boil. Once it's boiling, cover the pot and reduce the heat to low. Keep it at a low simmer and cook for 3 hours, stirring roughly every 30 minutes.

› When it's done, it should be a thick stew. The kidneys and liver will be tender and moist; the heart will be like braised pieces of short rib. The black-eyed peas will be slightly overcooked and bursting, which I like because it helps cream the stew out. Serve it by itself or over rice to your most adventurous friends—willing or not.

DOUBLE-CUT PORK CHOPS WITH CANE SYRUP GASTRIQUE

I love a big, beautiful, brined pork chop. The bigger the better—two of these chops will *easily* feed four people. This recipe calls for a double-cut chop, but I've also served triple-cut. Laying down that big of a piece of meat is a baller move. I like to keep things traditional by serving it with a hearty helping of Dirty Rice—hey, more meat! But then I get a little fancy with spoonfuls of Cane Syrup Gastrique. It's probably the number one dish we serve at the Meatery. | *Serves 4*

PORK CHOP AND BRINE
- 1 gallon water
- 1 cup dark brown sugar
- 1 cup kosher salt
- 2 tablespoons whole black peppercorns
- 4 bay leaves
- Ice (lots of it)
- 2 (20-ounce) bone-in double-cut pork chops (not frenched)

CANE SYRUP GASTRIQUE
- 1 cup cane syrup (or molasses)
- 1 cup cane vinegar (or cider vinegar)
- 4 tablespoons (½ stick) unsalted butter
- Dirty Rice (page 96), for serving
- Sliced green onions, for garnish

BRINE THE CHOPS

› Combine the water, sugar, salt, pepper, and bay leaves in a large pot and bring to a boil. Simmer for 20 minutes, then give it a good stir to make sure all the salt and sugar are dissolved. In a 3-gallon food-safe bucket, add the brine and enough ice until you have exactly 1½ gallons of brine.

› Once the brine is cold, place the pork chops in brine, cover, and refrigerate for 24 hours. Remove the chops from the brine and pat dry with paper towels. Season heavily with more salt and fresh ground black pepper.

MAKE THE GASTRIQUE

› In a saucepan, combine the cane syrup and cane vinegar. Bring to a boil over medium heat and cook until the liquid has reduced to 1 cup, about 20 minutes. There's no need to stir, but watch closely as it likes to burn. You can make this in larger batches, the shelf life is pretty much infinite. In a sealed jar, it does not need to be refrigerated.

GRILL THE CHOPS

› Preheat the grill to high. Preheat the oven to 400°F.

› Grill all sides of pork chops hard (even bone side) for 2 to 3 minutes on each side to get really hard grill marks. Put the pork chops in a roasting pan and top with 2 tablespoons butter each. Roast for 8 to 10 minutes, until 135°F internal temperature (for medium) or preferred temperature. Allow the chops to rest for 3 minutes in the pan. Then right before you serve, dip them on all sides in the juices and the butter that's left in the pan (a schmear).

› Serve immediately: Place the dirty rice on a platter, place the warm pork chops on top, and drizzle ¼ cup gastrique generously over the top of each. Garnish with sliced green onion. Serve family style. Fight over the bones.

BRAISED LAMB NECK WITH BRAISED BLACK-EYED PEAS

O ne day I had a lamb neck from somewhere and I thought, "Why not treat it like short ribs?" It has a lot of collagen and connective tissue, which means it makes the best sauce ever. With the red wine, anchovy, and Italian herb mix, it's an excellent braise—beautiful and simple. You can serve the whole dish as lamb neck braise like I do here, or tear it apart and make a lamb neck ragu with some mushrooms for an amazing pasta sauce. Where do you get a lamb neck? Special order it from your butcher. You will probably get a funny look. | *Serves 2*

1 (1½-pound) lamb neck

2 teaspoons kosher salt

2 teaspoons ground black pepper

1 teaspoon neutral vegetable oil, like canola or grapeseed

1 carrot, peeled and medium chopped

2 ribs celery, medium chopped

1 small onion, medium chopped

6 cloves garlic, smashed with a knife and roughly chopped

1 tablespoon fresh thyme, roughly chopped

1 tablespoon fresh rosemary, roughly chopped

1 tablespoon fresh oregano, roughly chopped

3 bay leaves

1 cup full-bodied red wine

1 anchovy filet, lightly smashed

2 tablespoons tomato paste

2 cups water

BRAISED BLACK-EYED PEAS

5 slices thick-cut bacon, cut into small pieces

1 medium white onion, diced

1 pound dried black-eyed peas

7 cups chicken stock (page 12 or store-bought)

3 bay leaves

1 teaspoon cayenne pepper

Kosher salt

Pickled Fennel (page 141), for serving

› Preheat the oven to 325°F.

› Season the lamb generously with the salt and black pepper.

› Heat a large Dutch oven over medium heat. Add the oil, then brown the lamb neck well on all sides to get a heavy sear. You want it nice and brown, 3 to 4 minutes on each side. Reduce the heat to low and remove the lamb neck from pan. Drain the pot, saving 1 teaspoon fat.

› Add the carrot, celery, and onion to the pot and sweat for about a minute. Add the garlic, fresh herbs, and bay leaves and sweat for about 2 minutes. Add the red wine and anchovy and bring up to a simmer. Add the tomato paste, stir well to make sure all the paste gets dissolved, and let simmer for about a minute.

Put the lamb back in the pot in the vegetable mixture and add the water. Cover with the lid or wrap tightly with foil. Transfer to the 325°F oven and bake for 4 hours, basting the lamb neck in its own juices once an hour, until fork tender.

MAKE THE BLACK-EYED PEAS

› While the lamb neck is braising, in a 4-quart pot over medium heat, sauté the bacon and onions for 2 to 4 minutes, stirring occasionally, until the bacon starts to render and the onions begin to soften. Add the black-eyed peas, stock, bay leaves, cayenne, and a large pinch of salt. Bring the peas to a boil then reduce to a simmer. Cook, covered, for 1 hour, until the peas are soft or bursting. Add salt to season to taste.

› When the lamb has finished cooking, skim the fat and discard it. This is one case where the more fat you remove, the better, even at the expense of losing some sauce. Lamb fat isn't really good at all, at least not in this dish.

› Put the braised black-eyed peas on the bottom of a serving plate and place the lamb neck on top. Cut a gash into the top of the neck and pour all of the cooking liquid on top; it should be pretty chunky and thick. (If the cooking liquid is loose like a gravy, reduce it in the pan until it's thick, like out-of-the-jar tomato sauce.) Mash the cooking liquid down into the gash of the lamb neck and cover the top of the lamb neck with the liquid. Garnish with a large pinch of pickled fennel and serve family style.

WHOLE ROASTED LEG OF LAMB

L ambs are often part of a modern boucherie. I like this dish because it's easy (and I love lamb). If it's your first lamb dish to cook, it's hard to mess it up. You can slightly undercook it. Mid-rare lamb? No big deal. And if you slightly overcook it, just add some red wine, cover it, and braise it down. It will still be dyn-o-mite. You've got a lot more leeway than if you were trying to perfectly cook lamb chops. Plus, it doesn't even need a sauce. The red wine brine pumps it with enough juice to keep it moist and flavorful. | *Serves 6 to 8*

BRINE AND LAMB

- 2 tablespoons picked fresh thyme (leaves picked off stem but not chopped)
- 2 tablespoons picked fresh rosemary (leaves picked off stem, but not chopped)
- 30 cloves garlic, peeled
- 1 large sweet onion, peeled
- 8 cups water
- 2 (750ml) bottles full-bodied red wine (like cabernet)
- 2 cups kosher salt

- 2 tablespoons whole black peppercorns, toasted
- 1 teaspoon crushed red pepper flakes
- 8 bay leaves
- Enough ice water (about 17 cups) to equal 3 gallons after simmering the brine mixture
- 1 (5-pound) bone-in lamb leg
- 20 cloves garlic, minced (buy a food processor and crack a beer, you don't want to mince all this garlic by hand)

- 2 teaspoons neutral vegetable oil, such as canola or grapeseed
- 5 teaspoons kosher salt
- 4 teaspoons finely ground black pepper

EQUIPMENT

4-gallon (or larger) food-safe container (you can get one at a restaurant supply store or online) or small cooler

Butcher twine, about 4 feet

BRINE THE LAMB

› Combine the thyme, rosemary, garlic, and onion in a food processor. Process until finely minced.

› In a 6-quart pot, combine the minced herb paste, water, red wine, salt, toasted black peppercorns, pepper flakes, and bay leaves. Bring to a boil. Reduce the heat to low and simmer, uncovered, for 20 minutes. In a food-safe vessel (4 gallons or larger), add the hot brine and about 17 cups ice water to get to *exactly* 3 gallons (48 cups) of liquid. Give the liquid a good stir (I use the lamb leg itself—why not?). Place the lamb leg in the brine. Cover and refrigerate for 24 hours, stirring again halfway through. A lot of the particulates will have settled, and all the good stuff will be at the bottom with the water from the melted ice on top.

› Remove the lamb leg from the brine and pat dry. Leave out for 2 hours to let the lamb come to room temperature.

ROAST THE LAMB

› Preheat the oven to 400°F.

› With a boning knife that is large enough that you can put a single finger into each hole, make 20 incisions 1 to 2 inches apart up and down the leg, all the way to the bone. Put approximately a clove's worth of minced garlic in each hole. Rub the lamb leg with the oil, salt, and black pepper.

› Take the large flap of flesh and skin from the bottom and fold it over to the ball in the joint of the leg, making it look like a uniform piece of meat. (Take the butt flap over the hip and attach it, treating the lamb like an amputee and making a knee covering.) Wrap it and tie it in place with butcher twine.

› On a large rimmed baking sheet that is large enough to accommodate the lamb leg (a large casserole dish would work as well), place the leg, cut side up (exposed part; if it was untrussed you'd be looking at the ball of the joint).

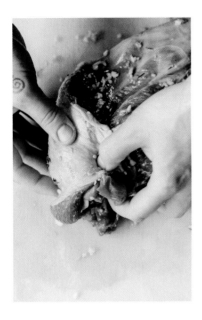 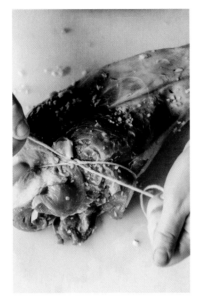 

› Roast in the 400°F oven for 45 minutes. Flip the leg and roast for another hour, or until the internal temperature is 135°F. Turn the oven off, but leave the lamb in for another 15 minutes. This allows for a hot rest so the meat will be rested and cooked evenly throughout, but will also still be warm when you put it on the table to serve.

› To serve, slice ¼-inch slices perpendicular to the bone, like a spiral ham, cutting against the grain. The thinner the slice, the better and more tender the lamb will be. The best parts are the charred garlicky crispy bits that have had the fuck roasted out of them.

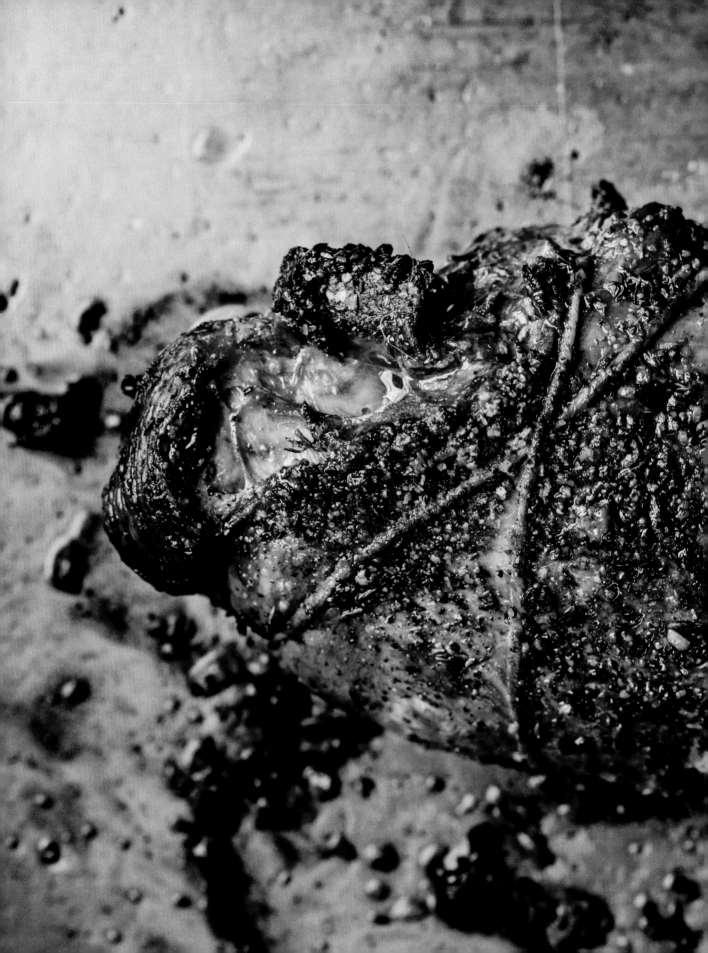

THE COMMUNITY TABLE

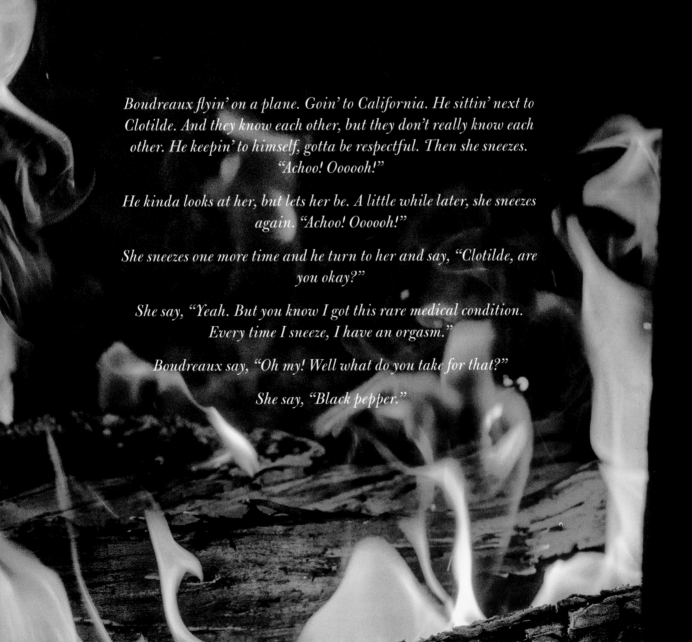

Boudreaux flyin' on a plane. Goin' to California. He sittin' next to Clotilde. And they know each other, but they don't really know each other. He keepin' to himself, gotta be respectful. Then she sneezes. "Achoo! Oooooh!"

He kinda looks at her, but lets her be. A little while later, she sneezes again. "Achoo! Oooooh!"

She sneezes one more time and he turn to her and say, "Clotilde, are you okay?"

She say, "Yeah. But you know I got this rare medical condition. Every time I sneeze, I have an orgasm."

Boudreaux say, "Oh my! Well what do you take for that?"

She say, "Black pepper."

We Cajuns would rather have people over to the house than go out to eat. We find any excuse to get together with friends, family, and people you think are your family but really aren't—like my uncle Buddy. He's just been friends with my dad since dental school.

Of course, I have my share of blood relatives. Daddy is the oldest of seven, Mama is the youngest of five. I've got uncles the same age as me and cousins who are as old as their uncles.

Don't worry, our family tree does have branches.

Daddy always said, "If you don't have two chickens, it's not worth making a gumbo." That means, why cook if you're not feeding a bunch of people? I grew up thinking everybody hosts crawfish boils and roasts a couple of pigs every year. The people who don't: What's wrong with y'all? We want to share, we want you to eat.

Cajun get-togethers are all-inclusive, rowdy affairs. The people you start the party with might not be the same ones left at the end. Kids go wild playing games or jumping into the pond. Women gossip in the house. Men gossip outside. Uncles play Liar's Poker (page 95). And the bar is always fully stocked.

There's a picture of me as a toddler holding a beer. I was knee-high when I had my first sip. And there's plenty of other stuff we did growing up that would get Child Protective Services called on parents today. Hell, it's a wonder I survived. We could do anything, so long as we were back before dark. I used to take Daddy's truck to buy him cigarettes when I was 13. One time I thought I was real cool and was gonna get me some too. I went in and said, "Um, a pack of Camels." The clerk said, "That's not what your daddy smokes. I'm calling him." Busted.

See, we do have *some* sense of order.

A crawfish boil is the event that brings a crowd together the most often. You can't just bust open a sack of crawfish and knock them down yourself. That's boring. So the first step in putting on a crawfish boil is: Get the beer. The second step is to get the crawfish. Third? Tell someone you've got beer and crawfish. The word will spread.

Everybody has their own way of boiling crawfish. Just like gumbo or fried chicken, there are generations of accumulated knowledge involved. You pick it up from your folks, and add your own riff. Here's one of my little additions: Sometimes I go gangbusters and put a gallon of whole garlic cloves in the boil for people to pick out of the pile of crawfish. Your breath might be a little rough afterward, but who gives a damn?

I've always got a playlist going that runs from Waylon Jennings to the Beastie Boys to the "Macarena." I love it when the music's playing. The kids are laughing. There's a chest full of beer. And everyone is standing around the table peeling and eating.

I've got nothing against tail meat, but if you're not busting the heads and sucking out that spicy juice, you're missing something essential to a crawfish boil. It's one thing to suck on the heads, it's another to crush them and really squeeze all the juice out. Just make sure you don't wear clothes you like too much. As a matter of fact, when you first get to a boil, you might as well go ahead and get baptized right off the bat. Pour a beer all over yourself, because it'll end up there anyway.

The other thing new crawfish boil initiates need to know is you wash your hands *before* you go to the bathroom and touch your ding-dong or your lady ding. That's because you've been putting your hands on a lot of spice. I always hear somebody crying from the bathroom and think, "Yeah, I told you." And if you want to have yourself some special sexual time after a crawfish boil—be careful, or it will be exactly as bad as you think. Ouchie ouchie. Lessons hard learned.

When my family lived out on the outskirts of Rayne, Louisiana, we had these old rice fields all around us. When they were flooded we would run down the sluice, ankle-deep in mud, and pick craw-fish. Wearing shorts and nothing else, we'd fill a five-gallon bucket for Daddy to boil up. The trick is grabbing the crawfish before it grabs you. If you get hold of the body just right, they can't reach around and grab you with their claws.

Ah yes, the old crawfish reacharound. That's a new move from Isaac. "Hey! That hurts! You pinched me!" Oh that? That's just my Crawfish Reacharound, baby.

BOILED CRAWFISH

You might not make your own boudin or fry your own cracklins, but you're just not a self-respecting Cajun if you can't boil crawfish. This is the most basic part of our repertoire. When crawfish season rolls around, we'll find any old excuse to stand around, shoot the shit, drink beer, and stuff our jaws. It might be the only time that some Cajuns shut up.

In my neck of the woods, there are restaurants that are open only part of the year and this is ALL they do. At Hawk's in Rayne, where I'm from, they've even come up with special tanks that aerate the crawfish and purge the hell out of them, removing any grit. (Gritty crawfish are awful. Don't skip the purging step below unless you want your friends to hate you.)

This recipe calls for cooking crawfish outdoors over a propane burner. You can cook crawfish inside on your stovetop, but you'd better not mind coughing up spice for a few days after. | *Serves 8 to 10*

---

1 large sack live crawfish (35 to 40 pounds)

12 gallons water (for cooking) and more for purging the crawfish

3 cups fresh-squeezed lemon juice

2 cups white wine vinegar

2 tablespoons Hondashi (see Note, page 83), optional

6 cups Isaac's Cajun Boil Spice (page 18) or Zatarain's Pro Boil, plus plenty more for serving

3 cups kosher salt, or more if needed

10 pounds small red potatoes (about 30 potatoes)

6 medium onions, peeled and halved lengthwise

10 bay leaves

8 ears of corn, shucked and broken in half

3 cups peeled whole garlic cloves, about 150 cloves

3 pounds hot smoked sausage, cut into 3- to 4-inch links

EQUIPMENT

3 coolers (two with hard sides and a bottom drain that hold at least 150 quarts each, and one that holds 48 quarts)

50-quart crawfish pot with basket, or the pot and basket of a turkey fryer

Propane burner

Newspaper, to cover the table

› Purge the crawfish to get the mud out of them: Empty the sack of crawfish into one of the large hard-sided coolers and fill with water until the crawfish are fully covered. Give a stir with a stick (or a long-handled spoon, whatever is close by) and let sit 3 minutes. Drain the water and repeat until water runs clear—it could be three times, it could be more than a dozen times, depending on how big and muddy the crawfish are. You can do this up to 4 hours before cooking.

› In the large crawfish pot, bring 12 gallons water to boil over a propane burner set to high.

› Meanwhile, in a large bowl, combine the lemon juice, vinegar, and, if using, Hondashi. You'll mix this with the cooked crawfish before you serve them. In another

small bowl, combine 2 cups of the lemon vinegar with 1 teaspoon from those 6 cups of boil spice and set aside; this is your Super Sauce to serve alongside the boiled crawfish.

› Once the water is boiling, add the salt and 3 cups of the boil spice. Taste the water to make sure it's as salty as seawater. If it's not, add more salt.

› Add the potatoes, onions, and bay leaves to the crawfish pot basket. Boil until the potatoes are beginning to soften, 10 to 13 minutes. Add the corn, garlic, and sausage. Cook until the potatoes are fork-tender, 7 to 10 more minutes. Once the potatoes are done, the rest will also be done, 17 to 23 minutes in total.

› Remove the vegetables from the basket, put them in the smaller cooler, and close the lid to keep warm. Bring that water in the crawfish pot back to a boil.

› Put the crawfish in the basket and submerge them in the boiling water. Cook for 7 to 8 minutes. The crawfish will become bright red and their tails will curl. Fish one out of the pot as a sacrifice to see if the batch is ready. Peel it; it should look like cooked lobster or shrimp. Remove the crawfish from the boiling water.

› Pour one-third of the crawfish back into the clean, unused large cooler, cover with about 1 cup of the remaining boil spice, and drizzle evenly with one-third of the lemon vinegar mixture (the one with no spice).

Repeat until all the crawfish are in the cooler. Close the lid. Give the cooler a few violent shakes.

› Transfer the cooked vegetables from the small cooler to the crawfish cooler and close the lid. After 5 minutes, give another violent shake. Repeat every 5 minutes for 20 minutes total.

› Cover a communal table with newspaper. Divide the lemon-vinegar-and-spice Super Sauce into little bowls and scatter them around the table for use as a dipping sauce. Place a mound of the boil spice at each person's spot for them to swipe peeled tails through; sometimes people just need a little more spice in their life. Then pour the crawfish out onto the newspaper and let people belly up.

CRAWFISH

When Mama was a girl, her dad would take the family to Cazan Lake and they'd stand on the levees between flooded rice fields dropping their nets. They'd set out 20 or so along the banks, catching 8 or 10 crawfish at a time. After a day out there, eating sandwiches off the hood of the car, they'd have buckets full of crawfish to take home and boil over an open fire.

When crawfish are in season (roughly February through May), every Cajun alive is boiling them. If I don't boil them at least once during the season, I feel like a sorry sonofabitch. And do not skimp on purging the crawfish. These fuckers live in the mud, so you've got to wash 'em with water until all grit and dirt is removed.

The best, and cleanest, crawfish in Louisiana can be found at Hawk's in Rayne. But if you're not lucky enough to live in this fine state, you can still get live crawfish. Try: Louisiana Crawfish Co. (lacrawfish.com), Cajun Grocer (cajungrocer.com), and Kyle LeBlanc Crawfish Farms (klcrawfishfarms.com).

ISAAC'S CRAWFISH BOIL MIX TAPE

Back in the High Life Again—Warren Zevon • *The Ballad of Curtis Loew*—Lynyrd Skynyrd • *Ballad of Gator McCluskey*—Charles Bernstein • *Bang Bang Bang Bang*—John Lee Hooker • *Bankrobber*—The Clash • *Big Boss Man*—Nancy Sinatra • *Black Betty*—Ram Jam • *Black Hole Sun*—Soundgarden • *Whiskey in the Jar*—Thin Lizzy • *Across the Universe*—Fiona Apple • *A Country Boy Can Survive*—Hank Williams, Jr. • *All Shook Up*—Elvis Presley • *Macarena*—Los del Rio • *Am I Free*—Wax Tailor • *And It Stoned Me*—Van Morrison • *Eye of the Tiger*—Survivor • *Anger Management*—Nathaniel Merriweather • *Arco Arena*—Cake • *Lake of Fire (Unplugged)*—Nirvana • *Don't Speak*—No Doubt • *Psycho Killer*—Talking Heads • *Monkberry Moon Delight*—Paul McCartney & Linda McCartney • *Roland the Headless Thompson Gunner*—Warren Zevon • *Those Were the Days*—Mary Hopkin • *Why Did You Do It?*—Stretch • *Back in the High Life Again*—Steve Winwood • *San Tropez*—Pink Floyd • *So What'Cha Want*—Beastie Boys • *The Man Who Sold the World*—Nirvana • *Theme from Rawhide*—Blues Brothers • *Father and Son*—Johnny Cash feat. Fiona Apple • *The Cisco Kid*—War • *Amanda*—Waylon Jennings • *When You're Hot, You're Hot*—Jerry Reed • *Women I've Never Had*—Hank Williams, Jr. • *Jolene*—Dolly Parton • *Louisiana Saturday Night*—Mel McDaniel • *I'm So Lonesome I Could Cry*—Hank Williams

BOILED CRABS

My dad taught me how to boil crabs. He likes the sweetness of crabs more than crawfish. He puts the crab traps in the water when we first get to our fish camp, pulls them up at the end of the day, and then we all gather around the table and go to town. It's one of the best communal breakings of bread on the bayou.

Eating crabs is one of the most animalistic things you can do. You take a whole animal and break it apart with your hands. I sometimes use my teeth. (It's a good thing Daddy is a dentist.) When you break it open, it looks like you're cracking into an alien. Until you get the hang of it, it can feel like a lot of work. But you're rewarded with the most amazing flavor, and when you pull out a big hunk of jumbo lump meat, you feel like a champ. | *Serves 10 to 12*

12 gallons water

6 cups Isaac's Cajun Boil Spice (page 18) or Zatarain's Pro Boil

1½ cups kosher salt

4 dozen live crabs

EQUIPMENT
50-quart crawfish pot with basket, or the pot and basket of a turkey fryer

Propane burner

Newspaper, to cover the table

› Fill a large pot with 12 gallons of water. Add the boil spice and salt to the water and bring to a boil. Put the live crabs in the boiling water. Bring it back up to a boil and cook for 15 minutes. Remove crabs from water and serve.

HOW TO EAT BOILED CRABS

Remove the claws from the crab and set them aside. Turn the crab face-up and remove the body from the carapace. Dig out any roe (aka "crab fat"). These golden nuggets will be in the middle of the body of female crabs. Scrape the lungs off the body with a butter knife. Then grab the crab by both sets of legs and break it in half. Grab one of the legs with one hand, and the body with the other, and turn the leg inward while holding the shell to remove the jumbo lump meat. For those claws: Using a claw cracker (or your mouth), crack the claws on all sides around the base and wiggle to remove the meat from the shell. See photos on the next page.

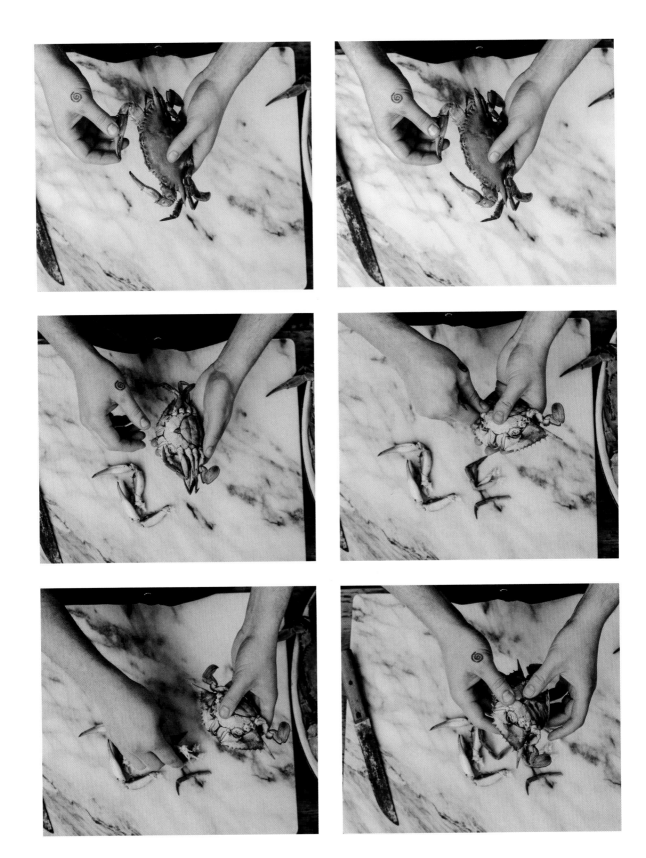

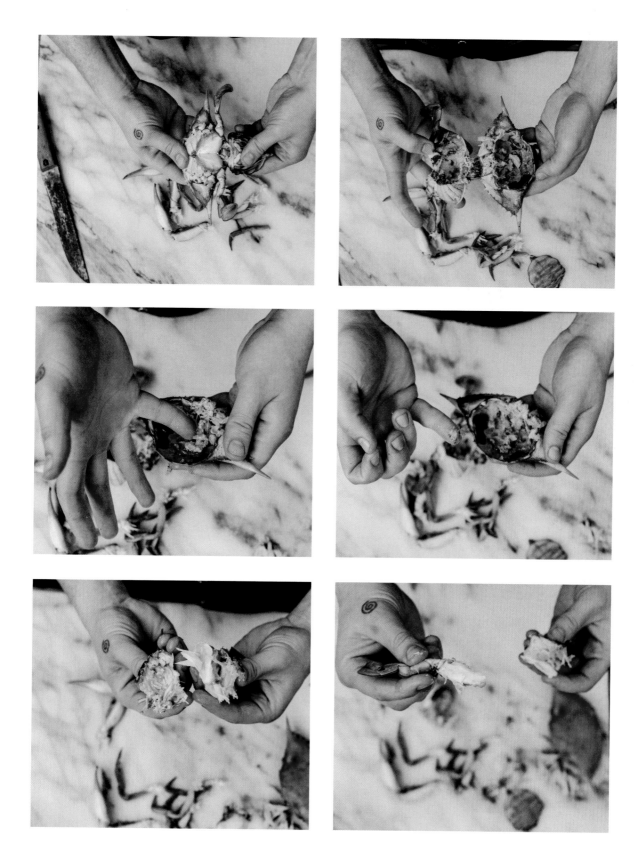

PEEL & EAT SHRIMP

Boiled shrimp are one of the easiest ways to feed a mess of people in a hurry. I figure around a half-pound per person—though, in Cajun country, you should probably figure a pound per head, because more folks always seem to show up whenever you throw shrimp on to boil. Here I split the difference and say 4 pounds will serve 6 people. I serve them with Cocktail Sauce (page 83) and Cane Vinegar Aioli (page 19).

My boiled shrimp always include celery salt. I had a cook once who was against using garlic powder, onion powder, celery salt—he said, "Why add powders if you want the flavor? Just add the actual ingredient." I agree—except for celery salt. There's something in there that isn't celery. I don't know what it is, and I don't want to know. But you can't get it anywhere else. | *Serves 6*

3 gallons water

3 cups white wine vinegar

1½ cups kosher salt

1½ cups sugar

24 bay leaves (truthfully, I just grab a big fistful)

36 cloves garlic, minced

3 tablespoons celery salt

1 tablespoon cayenne pepper

4 pounds head-on extra jumbo shrimp (about 16 to 20 per pound)

16 cups ice

EQUIPMENT

5-gallon stockpot

Note: If you can't get head-on shrimp, that's okay. Just make sure they have an intact shell.

› Put the water, vinegar, salt, sugar, bay leaves, garlic, celery salt, and cayenne in the 5-gallon stockpot and bring to a rolling boil over high heat. Once the water is boiling, add the shrimp and cook uncovered for 2½ minutes.

› Remove the shrimp using a spider or strainer and place in a large nonreactive mixing bowl. Add 4 cups of the poaching liquid and the ice and give it a good stir to disperse the ice throughout. I prefer my shrimp still warm, so I usually let the shrimp sit for just a minute, then drain and throw them out on the table for people to eat. (You can chill them all the way down in the ice and place the drained shrimp in the fridge if you prefer them cold.) But even when serving them warm, you *have* to shock them straight from the pot with the ice. If you don't, the shells will stick to the shrimp. And that's a big faux pas where I grew up.

BOILED SHRIMP FOR TWO

Here's how to do it on those nights when you want just a little boiled shrimp at home. | *Serves 2*

1 gallon water

1 cup white wine vinegar

½ cup kosher salt

½ cup sugar

8 bay leaves

12 cloves garlic, minced

1 tablespoon celery salt

1 teaspoon cayenne pepper

1 pound head-on extra jumbo shrimp (about 16 to 20 shrimp)

8 cups ice

› Follow the cooking instructions as above, using a 2-gallon pot instead of the huge stockpot. The method will be exactly the same.

SUPER SAUCE

Screw cocktail sauce. This vinegar mixture pumps up the flavor of boiled crawfish and crab better than anything else. My dad would put a small container of white distilled vinegar with cracked black pepper on the table at crawfish and crab boils. You dip the meat in and the high acid complements the fat of the meat. It's like a squeeze of lemon on fried fish. For Super Sauce, I follow the same idea, but use higher quality vinegar, add some lemon, and amp up the fish flavor with Hondashi. You make this as part of the crawfish boil (page 72), but here's a stand-alone recipe you can use with any seafood dish—anywhere you'd use cocktail sauce or mignonette. | *Makes 2½ cups*

1½ cups fresh-squeezed lemon juice

1 cup white wine vinegar

1 tablespoon Hondashi (optional)

1¼ teaspoons Isaac's Cajun Boil Spice (page 18) or Zatarain's Pro Boil

Note: If you've never tried Hondashi before, give it a try. It is fish-flavored MSG—instant freeze-dried dashi that comes as a grainy powder that you can find at most Asian markets and online—that gives a wonderful dose of umami and doubles down the concentration of fish flavor. I always keep it handy.

› In a small bowl, combine all the ingredients and whisk together. Divvy it up into bowls to place around the table. Dip peeled boiled crawfish, crabmeat, or shrimp into it.

COCKTAIL SAUCE

Okay, okay—I don't love cocktail sauce, but other people like it, so I make it. Once in a while the old stubborn chef gets put in check. There's enough horseradish here to wake up your nostrils. I like that. There's no sense in drowning your oyster or shrimp in cocktail sauce, so I make this strong enough for you to use just a little bit and still get the flavor. | *Makes 1¼ cups*

1 cup Heinz ketchup (Yes, Heinz is the best ketchup. No, they didn't pay me to say this.)

¼ cup hot prepared horseradish

1 teaspoon Worcestershire sauce

1 teaspoon hot sauce

1 teaspoon tequila blanco (either white or silver)

Grated zest and juice of 1 lemon

› In a small bowl, whisk all ingredients together until well combined. This will keep several days in the fridge, so feel free to make it ahead of time.

(When I make it, though, it's usually on the fly, with a fork in a soup bowl, for people who are already sitting at the table.)

MAW MAW TOUPS'
GULF SEAFOOD COUVILLION

This is my grandmother's seafood stew recipe. She was hell on wheels with a fishing pole. If she was making couvillion, she'd catch the fish and clean it herself. In fact, she liked fishing so much she stocked her swimming pool with fish to catch. No joke. It was a legit cement pond. Yeah, we're country.

She'd put a whole fish in this couvillion, usually speckled trout or redfish, scaled and gutted but with the head on. The fish would break down in the pot and thicken and season the broth. Once the fish fell apart, she knew the couvillion was done.

If you have a big enough pot, you can easily multiply the recipe. We've got a big ole family, so Maw Maw Toups was always doubling it—she never knew who might show up. | *Serves 6 to 8*

---

6 tablespoons (¾ stick) unsalted butter, divided

½ medium yellow onion, finely diced

1 small red bell pepper, finely diced

1 large rib celery, finely diced

1 teaspoon kosher salt

2 bay leaves

7 cloves garlic, minced

3 tablespoons all-purpose flour

½ cup tomato paste

¼ cup dry white wine

6 cups Easy Seafood Stock (page 15) or fish, crab, or shrimp stock

1 teaspoon picked and minced fresh thyme

½ teaspoon smoked paprika

½ teaspoon cayenne pepper

½ teaspoon ground white pepper

3 to 4 pounds mixed seafood (see Note)

Everyday Rice (page 17) or Crab Fat Rice (page 172), for serving

---

Note: I allow 6 to 8 ounces of seafood per person, in any combination of fish, peeled shrimp, and crabmeat. I prefer flaky white fish like speckled trout or redfish, either whole filets or filets cut into 2-inch slices. (Or you can do like Maw Maw Toups and put a whole gutted and scaled fish in.) The crab will break apart to thicken and season the stew, so don't splurge on jumbo lump; backfin or claw meat will work fine. Do pick through the crabmeat to remove any bits of shell. (I dip my fingers in a cup of water as I pick through the crab. The bits of shell sink to the bottom when you dip, so you don't flick it back into the crab.) For shrimp, go with peeled and deveined extra jumbo 16/20s (that is, 16 to 20 per pound). Ratio-wise, I tend to do equal parts by weight of fish and shrimp and go lighter on the crab because it's expensive.

› In a Dutch oven over medium heat, melt 2 tablespoons of the butter until it quits bubbling. Add the trinity (onion, bell pepper, celery), salt, and bay leaves, and cook until the onions are translucent, about 5 minutes. Add the garlic and sweat for 1 more minute. Remove the vegetables from the pan and reserve. Make sure you get all the vegetables out, but there's no need to wipe or clean the pan. There's still a lot of flavor in the fat that's left over.

› In the same Dutch oven over medium heat, make a brick roux (page 10), using the remaining 4 tablespoons butter and the flour and adding the tomato paste once the roux hits blonde. When the tomato paste begins to brown, add the vegetables back to the pot and stir.

› Add the wine and scrape the bottom of the pot with a wooden spoon until all the brown bits have come up. Add the stock, ½ cup at a time, stirring until fully incorporated after each addition. Add the thyme, paprika, cayenne, and white pepper, and stir.

› Bring the mixture up to a simmer over medium heat and cook uncovered for 45 minutes.

› Add the seafood and cook for 15 minutes, until the fish breaks apart easily. (If you are using a whole fish instead of fish filets, cook the fish for an hour, until it breaks

down, and add the rest of the seafood 15 minutes before it is done.)

› Adjust salt to taste and serve over Everyday Rice or Crab Fat Rice.

CRAWFISH BISQUE WITH STUFFED CRAWFISH HEADS

This dish is the most regal of crawfish dishes. But unless you have two grandmothers in the house, it's not getting made. It's tedious to stuff those crawfish heads and most people won't bother with it. Hell, even I hardly make it anymore. But you can also make this dish a lot simpler by doing away with the stuffed heads and just making the bisque. And because this all gets blended together, you can buy frozen Louisiana crawfish tail meat and not worry about it. It's also great with late-season crawfish, which are tougher, but their larger heads are easier to stuff. | *Serves 6*

7 tablespoons neutral vegetable oil, like canola or grapeseed, divided

2 ribs celery, minced

1 red bell pepper, minced

1 large onion, minced

8 cloves garlic, minced

1 jalapeño, stemmed, seeded, and minced

¾ cup brandy

6 tablespoons all-purpose flour

3 tablespoons tomato paste

3 quarts Crawfish Stock (page 15)

1 cup Louisiana jasmine rice

1 teaspoon ground Aleppo pepper (or paprika or crushed red pepper flakes)

1½ pounds cooked crawfish tail meat, peeled and deveined

Stuffed Crawfish Heads (recipe follows)

Kosher salt, to taste

Note: When I eat boiled crawfish, I eat the whole tail, vein and all. But when I cook with them, I remove the vein that runs down the backside. Every once in a while you find a gritty one, and that little bit of grit will ruin a bite.

› In a large cold skillet, combine 1 tablespoon of the oil, the celery, red bell pepper, onion, garlic, and jalapeño and gently sauté over medium heat for 3 minutes, or until the onions become translucent. Add the brandy and ignite with a long-handled lighter or by tipping the pan toward the flame of a gas stove. Watch out! Once the flame goes out, remove the pan from heat and set aside.

› In a large Dutch oven over medium heat, make a dark roux (page 10), using the remaining 6 tablespoons grapeseed oil and the flour, cooking until it is the color of milk chocolate, about 45 minutes. Once the roux is the right color, add the tomato paste and stir continuously for 1 minute, until the paste starts sticking to the pan. Add the stock in 1-quart increments, stirring constantly, until the liquid is fully incorporated into the roux. Add the sautéed vegetables, rice, and Aleppo pepper and bring to a simmer. Cook for 1 hour, stirring

occasionally. (While the stock is simmering, make your Stuffed Crawfish Heads.)

› Stir the cooked crawfish into the stock and bring back to a simmer. Immediately remove it from the heat. Carefully pour the bisque into a blender. If it doesn't all fit, blend it in batches. And make sure you don't fill the blender all the way to the top—as anyone with crawfish bisque on their ceiling already knows. Puree until smooth.

› Pour the pureed bisque back into the Dutch oven. If it's too thick—more gravy than bisque—add up to ½ cup water to thin. Gently lay the stuffed crawfish heads (or balls of stuffing) in the bisque. Do NOT stir. Turn the burner on low, bring it back to a simmer, and simmer for about 7 minutes, or until the internal temperature of the stuffed heads is 150°F.

› Before serving, season to taste. As a rule, I wait until the end to salt this dish: I usually use leftover crawfish seasoned from a crawfish boil, so I don't have to add any more salt. If you're making this from frozen crawfish tails or crawfish you've blanched just to make bisque, you'll need to add salt.

› Ladle the bisque into bowls, just under a cup per serving. Place a few stuffed heads in each bowl of bisque—more if you *really* like the person. The pecking order will decide how many heads each guest gets. Serve with a spoon for scooping bisque and a cocktail fork for picking the stuffing out of the heads.

STUFFED CRAWFISH HEADS

- 5 ounces crawfish tail meat (about 1 cup packed)
- 1 bunch green onions (about 7), green tops only, thinly sliced
- 3 ounces fatback, cubed (You can also use the fatty part—the top cap—of pork belly, or pork butt, or pancetta—you get my drift; if you're desperate you could use the fatty part of a pork chop. I prefer not to use bacon because it's a little smoky.)
- 2 tablespoons heavy cream
- ½ teaspoon kosher salt
- ½ teaspoon ground black pepper
- 21 cleaned crawfish heads (or what you have left over from picking the tail meat for the bisque)

Note: You can save time by forming the stuffing into balls, and not stuffing the heads. If you don't have pastry bags, don't fret. Get yo'self a ziplock bag. Press all of the stuffing mixture into one corner of the bag and squeeze to get the air out. Cut off the tip of that corner, creating a hole about ½ inch wide.

› Combine all the ingredients except the crawfish heads in a food processor and process for 10 seconds. The mixture should be the consistency of a crumbly paste when done. Use immediately, while still cold. If you're making this in advance of stuffing the crawfish heads, put the stuffing mixture in the fridge until ready to fill the heads (or roll into balls).

› Pry open a crawfish head a little bit where it was previously attached to the body—not all the way, just enough to open it up. Using a pastry bag, pipe the cold crawfish head stuffing into the head. When all the heads are full, give the stuffing a little pat to tuck it well into each head. Roll any extra stuffing into little balls. Refrigerate them all until ready to cook in the bisque.

CRAWFISH CORNBREAD DRESSING

I call this dressing. You call it what you want. But we'll both agree that it's delicious. Mama warms up her cornbread and her sauce, then folds in her cornbread and it's done. It's probably not a true dressing, but I don't care. It's awesome. We bake it just to get crispy bits on the edges, not to cook it through. I prefer to use fresh crawfish meat, but since the dressing is creamy and you won't notice the odd texture that frozen crawfish can get, frozen will do. You'll see the dressing at Thanksgiving even when you know there's not a fresh crawfish to be found. | *Serves 8 to 10*

- 2 tablespoons unsalted butter, divided
- 1 medium onion, finely diced
- 1 red bell pepper, finely diced
- 1 rib celery, finely diced

- 5 cloves garlic, minced
- 1 pound cooked crawfish tail meat
- 1½ teaspoons kosher salt
- ¼ teaspoon finely ground black pepper

- ¼ teaspoon cayenne pepper
- 2 cups Crawfish Stock (page 15), or any seafood stock
- 5 cups crumbled Isaac's Cornbread (page 134, about half a recipe)

› Preheat the oven to 400°F.

› In a large Dutch oven, melt 1 tablespoon of the butter over medium heat. Add the onion, bell pepper, and celery and cook for 10 minutes, stirring occasionally. After 10 minutes, the trinity should start to brown a little bit—this is intentional; you want it more than just translucent—you want it thoroughly softened and beginning to brown. Since we're not braising this dish down, you really want to have your trinity cooked—I don't like crunchy trinity. Stir in the garlic and cook for another minute.

› Stir in the crawfish, salt, black pepper, and cayenne. Add the stock. While still over medium heat, slowly bring the mixture to a low simmer then remove from the heat. Add the remaining 1 tablespoon butter and stir until it's fully melted. Once the butter has melted, gently fold in the crumbled cornbread until it's well incorporated, being careful not to smush it all to bits.

› Scoop the mixture into a 9 x 13-inch casserole dish and spread out evenly. Bake for 10 minutes, or until the edges are browned. Call your Cajun mother and thank her.

COCHON DE LAIT

In Cajun country, a *cochon de lait* refers both to a suckling pig—literally a "pig of milk," fresh off the teat, about 30 pounds—and the experience of getting together to roast a pig of any size. Growing up, there was always a cochon de lait thrown by my mother's family, the Carts. It was (and still is) a big to-do, with the whole family showing up with 30 side dishes and 10 desserts. There'd always be live music, an accordion or a fiddle or two, kids running around, uncles lying, and grandmothers gossiping. For the big gatherings, we cook a 100-pound pig instead of a suckling. The pig cooks overnight, and traditionally someone stays up all night to watch it. But the alcohol flows. So you also need someone to watch the watcher. In all my years, I've never seen anyone burn the pig.

For the big gathering, you start by digging a 4- to 5-foot-deep trench that's as long and wide as the pig you're going to cook. You build a roaring fire and let it burn down to embers. And then you hoist the pig onto a spit about 6 to 8 feet above the embers. It cooks low and slow, starting with the cut side down. Then you rotate it on the spit to skin side down and fill the body cavity with onions and garlic in the sizzling fat (some of the best bites at a cochon de lait).

I've adapted the traditional cochon de lait to use an actual suckling pig so you can cook it in your oven at home. So if you don't want to take the time to dig a pit and put a pig on a spit, but still want to roast a whole pig to feed a crowd, here you go. For Thanksgiving. For Christmas. Or just 'cause it's fun. | *Serves 12 to 16*

BRINE AND PIG

- 101 cloves of garlic (you can use just 100 cloves, but I say 101 because I like being cute; about 2 cups)
- 6 apples, cored and quartered
- 2 large onions, quartered
- 6 jalapeños, stemmed and cut into 1-inch circles, seeds included
- 4 cups kosher salt
- 1 pound dark brown sugar
- 1 cup honey
- 6 (12-ounce) bottles dark or amber-style beer
- 2 gallons water
- 3 gallons ice water
- 1 suckling pig (about 30 pounds), head and feet on, gutted, scalded, and shaved
- Ice (lots of it)

SEASONING
- ½ cup kosher salt
- ½ cup finely ground black pepper

EQUIPMENT
- 120-quart cooler (make sure it's big enough to fit your pig and is *very* clean)

BRINE THE PIG

› In a large food processor, in batches, buzz up the garlic, apples, onions, and jalapeños for 30 seconds; it should be the consistency of cheap restaurant salsa. Transfer the mixture to a large stockpot and add the salt, brown sugar, honey, beer, and water. Bring the mixture to a boil over high heat. Once boiling, reduce the heat and simmer for 20 minutes. Remove from the heat and pour into the 120-quart ice chest. (Don't forget to plug up the weep hole first, you idiot. Yes, of course

I've forgotten that. Everyone has.) Add the 3 gallons ice water on top of the hot liquid. Mix well.

› Crack the pig's rib cage on the inside near the spine: Using a heavy cleaver, score each of the pig's rib bones near the spine, striking down like you're pounding in a nail with the blade. Once all the rib bones are scored, spread the rib cage flat and press down to unfold the ribs. This will make one of the most metal sounds ever.

› Submerge the pig in the ice chest in brine. Wash the pig well in the brine, using your hands to splash it in the nostrils, the ears, in the chest cavity. Submerge 3 or 4 large kitchen towels in the brine, draping them over any exposed parts of the pig. Keeping the ice chest in a cool area, place three 1-gallon ziplock bags of ice in the cooler. Once the ice melts, replace it. As long as the ziplock bags don't break, they won't dilute the brine.

› Refrigerate in this way for 48 hours. Halfway through, flip the pig and reposition the brine-soaked towels to make sure no parts are left exposed to air.

› Remove the pig from the brine. Wring the towels dry and use them to wipe off excess brine.

ROAST THE PIG

› Preheat the oven to 350°F.

› Generously rub the salt and pepper all over the pig. Place the pig splayed side down on an extra-large baking sheet, preferably one with at least a 2-inch rim. To make it all fit in your oven, you may have to remove the hind- and forefeet. If you don't, don't. But if you do, they should easily come off with a butcher knife and a couple of twists.

› Roast for 2 hours and 20 minutes total, or until the internal temperature reaches 155°F, rotating the tray halfway through.

› Remove from oven and lightly drape with aluminum foil. Let rest for 20 minutes.

› When you go to pick the pig, the skin cracklins will be the best part. The meat just underneath the belly ribs is divine perfection—imagine creamed pork. Mmmmmm.

CAJUN MICROWAVE

The Caja China is commonly referred to as a Cajun microwave or a hot box. It's a portable wooden or metal box that you can cook a whole pig (or turkey or lamb or goat) in. I don't know if we Cajuns stole it from China or Mexico, but we definitely didn't invent it. We sure as hell love to use it, though—it's a magical box that lets you cook a pig anywhere you go.

Normally roasting a whole animal would be a multi-day affair—building the pit, erecting the spit, building a fire, roasting the animal, and cleaning it all up—but with the hot box, you can do it in a day. You put the pig in cold, resting on a grate just raised off the bottom of the box, put the lid on it, build a fire with wood or coals on top, light it, and you're cooking. For a suckling pig of 30 pounds, it'll take roughly 3 to 4 hours, until the pig's internal temperature reaches 155°F. For a 100-pounder, figure on 5 to 6 hours. Just keep the coals going on top until you're done.

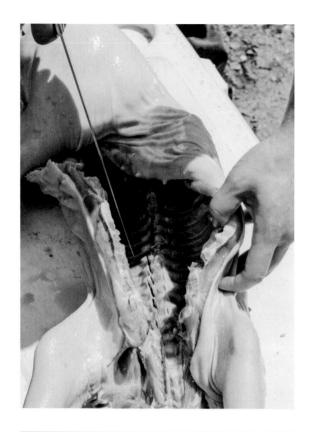

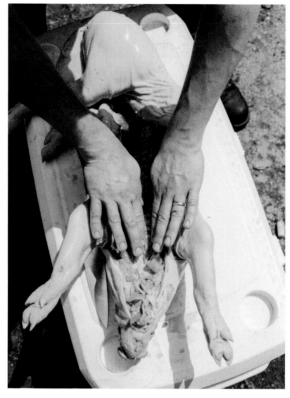

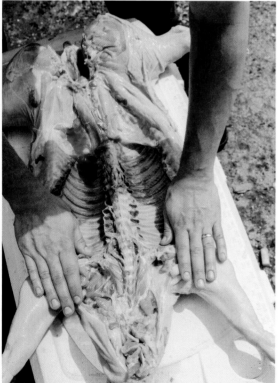

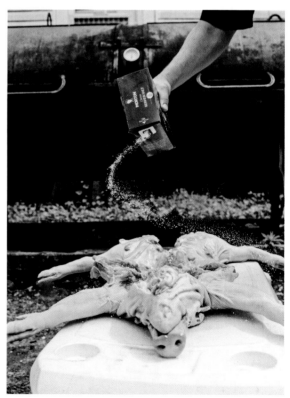

LIAR'S POKER

Everyone pulls out a dollar bill. You look at the serial numbers on one side. Then you play by loose poker rules: pairs, three of a kind, four of a kind, five of a kind. Zeros are tens. There are no straights on two pairs or anything like that, just multiples of a single number. The trick is to outbid your opponent. I'll start and say, "I have two 7s," and you have to say something higher than that—three 7s or three 4s or three whatevers.

Now, you can lie. But if I call you out on your lie, you lose. So if I say I have two 7s and you don't think I do, you say "call." You keep bidding higher until someone calls. If the person who was called was bidding honestly, they win the money. If they were lying, the person who called wins.

Liar's Poker is a quick game, and it's great with single dollar bills. But sometimes I see the uncles playing with hundred-dollar bills and think, "Hold on, guys."

DIRTY RICE

Dirty rice is as common at the Cajun table as mashed potatoes and gravy is elsewhere. It's the meatiest, richest rice dish you'll ever eat, and it gets its color, its dirtiness, from glorious, glorious meat. The trick to this dish is getting a good char on the ground beef. I like to use ground sirloin, keeping it in a block and searing it like I would a steak before the meat is broken up and braised. That caramelized meat makes the difference between a good pot of dirty rice and something you'd be embarrassed to serve a Cajun grandmother.

Just before you combine the meat mixture with the rice, you've basically got a dark roux chili. If you added some fresh tomato and cooked it down until it's nice and tight, you'd have a killer ragu for an incredible lasagna. You can make the meat part of the Dirty Rice ahead of time and freeze it for up to 6 weeks. | *Serves 4 to 6*

MEAT

- 1 (1-pound) block lean ground sirloin
- 2 teaspoons kosher salt
- 1 tablespoon grapeseed oil
- ½ teaspoon ground black pepper
- ½ teaspoon toasted ground cumin
- ¼ teaspoon cayenne pepper
- ⅓ cup amber beer

GRAVY

- ¼ cup grapeseed oil
- ¼ cup all-purpose flour
- ½ cup finely chopped white onion
- ½ cup finely chopped green bell pepper
- ⅓ cup finely chopped celery
- 4 cloves garlic, crushed
- ⅓ cup amber beer

- 1 cup chicken stock (page 12 or store-bought), plus more as needed
- 2 cups Everyday Rice (page 17)
- 2 tablespoons unsalted butter
- ½ bunch green onions (green tops only), chopped

Kosher salt

SEAR THE MEAT

› Season the block of sirloin—no fancy shaping needed, just use it how it comes out of the tray from the grocery store—with 1 teaspoon of salt on each side.

› In a large skillet, heat the oil over medium-high heat until it starts to smoke. Place the sirloin block in the skillet in one piece and let it sear until it really browns and caramelizes, 3 to 5 minutes. Then flip it and repeat, 3 to 5 minutes longer. Let it do its thing.

› Once the block of sirloin is well seared, chop it up in the pan with a metal spatula to sear the inside bits. Add the black pepper, cumin, and cayenne and stir well. Cook for a minute. Add the beer to deglaze the pan, and cook 1 minute longer, scraping up any browned bits. Remove from the heat and set aside. At this point, you could freeze the meat.

MAKE THE GRAVY

› In a heavy Dutch oven over medium heat, make a dark roux (page 10) using the oil and flour, about 45 minutes. Once it's the color of milk chocolate, add the onion, bell pepper, and celery and stir together. Cook for a minute. Stir in the garlic and cook for 1 minute longer. Add the beer and mix well. In 1/3-cup increments, add the stock, stirring well between each addition. Stir frequently, but not continuously, until you have a well-emulsified gravy, thick enough to coat the back of a spoon.

› Once the gravy is done, add the cooked beef. Add a splash of stock to the meat pan to deglaze to get the remaining "junk" out—the delicious extra bits that stick to the pan—and add to the gravy and meat. Bring the meat and gravy mixture back to a bare simmer. Cover and cook for 1½ hours, or until the raw flour has all cooked out and the sauce has no chalky or floury flavor.

TO SERVE

› Add the cooked rice, butter, and green onions to the meat gravy in the pot. Stir it all together over low heat, just to warm it all through. Add salt to taste and serve.

BETTER THAN POPEYES

The other night, my daughter Poppy was throwing a fit over the dirty rice I served her. Why? Because it didn't look like the dirty rice from Popeyes. Amanda went over to her and calmly but authoritatively said, as only Amanda can, "Now, your daddy is a great cook. He taught Popeye how to make that rice. So you should eat what he served you."

TATA BOUILLE
(MAW MAW TOUPS' TARTE À LA BOUILLE)

At its most basic, you could call this a custard pie. It's my grandmother's take on *tarte à la bouille,* a custard pie with a sweet crust, but our French is awful so it became *Tata Bouille.* I didn't know her version wasn't traditional until much later in life…like when I started working on this cookbook. The traditional version typically has a top and bottom sweet crust, but my grandmother would just make a single crust that she draped over the edges of whatever vessel she was cooking in, and then folded it over the top, leaving some of the custard exposed. Hers also had alcohol in it. We're definitely related.

This was a dessert for special occasions, but Maw Maw Toups could knock it out easily—in a casserole dish, for crying out loud. I don't have a sweet tooth (I have an alcoholic tongue instead), so I don't eat a lot of dessert, but you can bet your ass I tear into this whenever it's around.

When we have extra dough left over from the crust, we roll it out, cut it up, and bake it off like cookies. We call them boat cookies because they are the perfect thing to take out fishing for a little boat snack. | *Makes one 10-inch pie*

PIE DOUGH
- 2½ cups all-purpose flour
- 2½ teaspoons baking powder
- 1 cup granulated sugar
- 4 tablespoons (½ stick) unsalted butter, cut into ¼-inch dice and frozen
- ¼ cup whole milk
- 1 large egg plus 1 egg yolk
- 1 teaspoon vanilla extract

FILLING
- 1 cup Southern Comfort
- ½ cup granulated sugar
- 5 tablespoons cornstarch
- 3 cups heavy cream
- 1 teaspoon vanilla extract

MAKE THE DOUGH

> In a food processor, combine the flour, baking powder, and sugar and pulse 3 or 4 times. Add the frozen butter, all at once, and pulse another 10 times, until the mixture looks crumbly like sand. Put the whole food processor bowl into the fridge and chill until ready to use.

> In a medium mixing bowl, whisk together the milk, whole egg, egg yolk, and vanilla until well mixed.

> Remove the crumbly flour mixture from the refrigerator and pour it into a large mixing bowl. Make a well in the center of the bowl by pushing the flour mixture to the edges. Pour the milk and egg mixture into the center well. Using your first two fingers, slowly incorporate the flour mixture into the egg mixture by starting with the flour closest to the egg, and working more and more into the egg mixture. If you've ever

made homemade pasta, it's the same process. As the ingredients begin incorporating, mix them using your whole hands. Mix quickly; you don't want to overwork the flour or let the butter melt. Eventually, the flour and egg mixture will form a loose and shaggy ball of dough. On a floured work surface, knead the dough about 6 times to make sure everything is well incorporated. Form it into a ball. Wrap it in plastic wrap and chill it in the fridge for 30 minutes.

> You can make the dough ahead of time and refrigerate it for 3 days or freeze it for up to a month. If you freeze it, give it a day to defrost in the fridge before using it.

MAKE THE FILLING

> In a small saucepan over medium-low heat, reduce the Southern Comfort for about 30 minutes, until you are left with about 1 tablespoon. You don't need to stir

this at all. It might ignite if you bring it up to heat too quickly. But it doesn't matter if it flames off or not—just watch your hair. Once reduced, set it aside and let cool to room temperature.

› In a small mixing bowl, whisk the sugar and cornstarch together.

› In a small saucepan over medium heat, bring the cream to a simmer (or as a pastry chef would say, scald it). No need to stir this, either. Right when it starts to simmer (should take about 15 minutes), gradually whisk in the sugar mixture. Once that is well combined, add the vanilla and Southern Comfort reduction. Stir well to combine and remove from the heat.

MAKE THE PIE
› Preheat the oven to 350°F.

› Remove the dough from the fridge. Dust a flat surface—ideally a cold one like stainless steel or stone—and rolling pin well with flour. With the rolling pin, roll out the dough to a 14-inch diameter, about ¼ inch thick throughout (a little thicker than a normal pie crust).
› Once the dough is rolled out, roll it onto the rolling pin and then unroll it into a 10-inch cast iron skillet or

10-inch pie pan. Gently press the dough to mold it into the pan. Extra crust will drape over the edges.

› Pour the custard filling into the dough in the skillet. Fold the edges of dough over the top. They won't meet in the center. If you have extra dough left after rolling it out, you can put it on top in the center, but it's not necessary. I just like how it looks when you crown it like that. (Or you can use the extra dough to make the aforementioned boat cookies. It's always a good time to go fishing.)

› Bake for 25 to 30 minutes, until the top is golden brown and the custard filling is set. Let rest for 20 minutes. You can do the whole windowsill thing if you want, but never in my life have I ever seen a pie actually rest on a windowsill.

› Serve it warm, scooped out with a spoon like a cobbler. We never slice Tata Bouille. Or, you could let it cool down in the fridge and eat it chilled, which is normally how we do it.

CANE SYRUP HAND PIES

This recipe came from my Maw Maw Cart, but it's my variation. Well, my variation, thanks to the help of my mother-in-law, Janis. Maw Maw Cart didn't write down the recipe, but Janis, who is a far more talented baker than I am, helped me chase the taste memory. (Bless her.) If you're related to me and reading this, and you have Maw Maw's actual recipe, can you send it over?

There was a split in the family about whether to have nuts or not, so Maw Maw Cart made them both with and without. I'm on the no-nut side. I don't like nuts in pastries. In ice cream, I love them. But put a pecan in a cookie and you can go fuck yourself. | *Makes about 24 pies*

FILLING

- 2 cups granulated sugar, divided
- ½ cup water
- 6 tablespoons (¾ stick) unsalted butter
- ½ cup heavy cream
- 2 teaspoons vanilla extract, divided
- 2 dashes fine sea salt, divided
- 2 cups cane syrup
- 6 large eggs, beaten

HAND PIE DOUGH

- 4 cups all-purpose flour
- 1 tablespoon kosher salt
- 2 teaspoons granulated sugar
- 4 sticks (1 pound) unsalted butter, frozen and cut into ½-inch pieces
- ¾ cups ice water (make a large glass of ice water to measure from)

TO ASSEMBLE

Egg wash of 1 large egg and 2 tablespoons heavy cream beaten together

Pure cane sugar, to garnish

EQUIPMENT

12-cup food processor

Silicone baking mat (or parchment paper), dusted with all-purpose flour

Large baking sheets

Rolling pin, dusted with all-purpose flour

Pastry brush

Parchment paper

1½-inch cookie dough scoop (or you can use a large tablespoon)

Note: Cane syrup is a Louisiana staple. It's typically thicker than maple syrup, more like molasses, and it's what we *always* had on pancakes and waffles.

MAKE THE FILLING

› Preheat the oven to 350°F. Grease a 9 x 13-inch casserole dish with butter. In a small heavy saucepan over medium heat, combine 1 cup of the granulated sugar and the water and bring to boil, stirring regularly until all the sugar is dissolved. Remove from the heat and stir in the butter and then the cream. Mix well and add 1 teaspoon of the vanilla and a dash of sea salt. Pour the mixture into a large bowl and let cool.

› Add the remaining 1 cup sugar, remaining 1 teaspoon vanilla, the cane syrup, beaten eggs, and dash of sea salt. Stir until well blended. Pour into the buttered casserole dish and bake for 30 minutes, turning the casserole dish halfway through to ensure the filling cooks evenly. Let cool.

› Pour the mixture into a bowl and remix the filling. Cover and store in the refrigerator for several hours (overnight is better), until the filling is completely cold and set.

MAKE THE PIE DOUGH

› Combine the flour, kosher salt, and granulated sugar in a food processor and pulse until blended. Add one-third of the frozen butter pieces at a time and pulse. Open the processor and fluff with a fork as needed. The mixture should look crumbly, but not creamed.

› Turn on the food processor and quickly drizzle in the ice water. As soon as the water is incorporated (this will happen very quickly), stop the processor.

› Empty the mixture out onto a floured silicone baking mat. I use a baking mat that has crust sizes printed on it. This comes in handy when you are rolling out lots of 6-inch pie crusts. Press the dough mixture into a ball, very quickly so the heat from your hands doesn't melt the butter. Once you have a ball of dough, wrap it in plastic wrap and place it in a ziplock bag. Put it in the refrigerator for several hours (overnight is better) until the dough is completely cold and set.

ASSEMBLE THE HAND PIES

› Line a large baking sheet with parchment paper.

› Remove the dough and filling from the refrigerator. Using a sharp knife, slice off a chunk of the dough, enough to roll into a 1½-inch ball. Flatten the dough on the floured silicone baking mat and roll into a 6-inch circle with the floured rolling pin.

› With your pastry brush, brush the outer edges of the dough circle with egg wash. Using the cookie dough scoop, put two scoops (about two heaping tablespoons) filling into the center of the dough. Fold the dough over in half and seal by crimping the edges with a fork.

› Place the pie on a lined baking sheet. Repeat rolling and filling until the baking sheet is filled, being careful not to crowd the hand pies. Place it in the refrigerator for 30 minutes.

› Preheat the oven to 350°F. Remove the pies from refrigerator and, using a sharp knife, cut 3 slits into the top of each pie. Brush each pie with the egg wash and sprinkle cane sugar on top.

› Bake for 35 minutes, or until golden brown. Let cool for 20 minutes before serving warm; they're also good at room temp the next day.

THE HOMESTEAD

Boudreaux had been up all night drinking at da bar.
Drinking dat Dixie beer. Just slammin' 'em back.

He come home 'bout one o'clock in da mornin'. And who sittin' on da
front? Clotilde. She pissed at him. She grab him by da ear and take
him all da way down to da Dixie brewery..

She say, "Look, dey can make dis beer faster than you can
drink it."

He say, "Yeah, but I got 'em workin' nights."

My mama's side, the Carts, were hardworking people. They dug rice canals, picked cotton, sewed their own clothes, and did odd jobs like cutting down trees and hauling wood. They worked hard because they had to, and they could make *anything* out of nothing. That was especially true for food.

Maw Maw Cart could go into the woods and find every edible plant within a mile. She kept fig trees in the backyard and made fig preserves. If someone caught a turtle, she'd cook it. Turtle eggs, too. They kept chickens. And they always had gardens full of tomatoes, squash, beans, watermelons, peppers, collards, turnips, radishes, fresh herbs, and flowers. My parents still keep gardens today—two of them. Because Mama won't let Daddy near hers. (I don't blame her.)

My grandparents, Eva and Lester, grew up without refrigeration, so they were experts at preserving food: pickling, salting, canning, smoking, curing, and drying everything from vegetables to meat. If they had a good year in the garden, they picked the harvest and put it up for leaner months, or shared it with their neighbors. Meat was precious. When Maw Maw Cart was raising five kids, she didn't always have enough money to buy meat. So she'd make long gravies to stretch what they did have. Paw Paw Cart, the breadwinner, might get a piece of meat at supper, but my mama and her brothers and sisters got roux-enriched gravies over rice, seasoned with pan drippings.

One time, after my parents got married, Mama and Daddy were driving to my grandparents' house and met a man alongside the road with a bunch of chickens. The man's dog had gotten into his neighbors' chickens while they were out of town and killed them. Rather than let the meat go to waste, he was flagging folks down to give it away. My dad went into the yard and gathered as many chickens as he could carry and took them to Maw Maw Cart. She immediately took them to the backyard and started burning the feathers off and gutting them. That's good eatin'!

There was no meal in the Cart home like Sunday dinner—we call it dinner, not lunch. Sundays back then were for church and visiting family. After Mass, everyone would congregate at my grandparents' house, or at an aunt or uncle's house, around a mess of food. Even in the leanest times, they managed to feed a crowd.

When you walk into a Cajun house, there are things that just always happen. You will be offered a drink. You will be fed. Most of our meals are eaten at the house. Even today, when we go visit, Mama is offended if we say, "Let's go out." The first question you get asked when you walk in my mama's house is, "Are you hungry?" People ask me about the dining scene back home. I have no clue. Hospitality is in our bones, whether we've got much to share or not. There was a train track that ran behind the house and Maw Maw Cart would even come up with something to feed the hobos—the bona fide kind with an actual bandana on a stick—who showed up at the back door. She never turned anyone away. Though the hobos did have to stay on the back stoop.

After Sunday dinner, my mama's family would break out the fiddles and guitars and drag the furniture to the edges of the living room to create a dance floor. Mama would crawl under a bench and watch all the feet two-stepping around. My grandparents have both passed on, but they danced right up until the end. Every weekend, even at ages 83 and 90, they'd pack a little flask of salty dogs, get in the car, with Maw Maw Cart driving, and hit up a Cajun dance hall where bands like Joe Simon or Aldus Broussard and the Louisiana Cajuns were playing.

I grew up a little differently. We cooked and ate the way we did more out of tradition than necessity. My father was a dentist, a busy man, a workaholic. But he liked to garden and hunt and fish. He didn't make pickles or beef jerky because he *had* to. He made them because he liked it. It put him closer to the land. That connection to where you come from is a Cajun mentality instilled early on. He made me shovel pig shit for years. We had a pig, horses, geese, ducks, chickens, dogs, cats—a little bit of everything. Again, we didn't have a farm out of necessity. But to Daddy, it was important, and he expected us to work and earn our keep. I guess that's why my work ethic is what it is today.

Quite frankly my dad's pickles probably cost more than a jar at the store, given the cost of his tractor and his time. But to us, buying pickles is no fun. I continue to make my own pickles and hot sauce and jams because I like it. It makes me feel Cajun. It reminds me where I came from.

GUMBO #1
CHICKEN AND SAUSAGE GUMBO

This is Gumbo 101: the first gumbo you learn in the Cajun kitchen. I couldn't tell you the first time I made this with my mom because I've had my hands in it since I could walk. It's the easiest one to find ingredients for and you can feed a bunch of people easily by doubling, tripling, or quadrupling the recipe. It's surely the most popular gumbo on the planet.

No matter how much you might be tempted to, do not skim the little oil slick of chicken fat off the top of your gumbo. Taste that! That's what rice is for, to soak all that flavor up. My gumbo comes out rich, and God, it's delicious. | *Serves 4*

- 4 bone-in, skin-on chicken thighs
- 3 teaspoons kosher salt, divided
- 2 teaspoons ground black pepper, divided
- ½ cup grapeseed oil
- ½ cup all-purpose flour
- 1 large onion, diced
- 1 large red bell pepper, diced
- 2 ribs celery, diced
- 10 cloves garlic, crushed
- 4 bay leaves
- 1 (12-ounce) bottle amber-style beer
- 5 cups chicken stock (page 12 or store-bought)
- ½ teaspoon cayenne pepper
- 1 pound andouille sausage (or your favorite smoked sausage), cut into bite-size pieces (½-inch half-moons)
- Everyday Rice (page 17), for serving
- Sliced green onions, for garnish
- Issac's Pepper Paste of Pain (page 21), optional

› Preheat the oven to 400°F. Season the chicken thighs with 2 teaspoons of the salt and 1 teaspoon of the black pepper. Place on a rimmed baking sheet, skin side up, and roast for 20 minutes, or until the skin is lightly browned. Remove from the oven and set aside. Don't throw that fat away, it's going in the gumbo later.

› In a heavy Dutch oven over medium heat, make a dark roux (page 10), using the oil and flour, about 45 minutes. Once the roux is the color of milk chocolate, add the trinity of onion, bell pepper, and celery, and stir once every 5 seconds for about a minute until the vegetables begin to soften and caramelize. The roux is rocking hot, so these vegetables are going to cook really quickly. Don't walk away! After a minute, add the garlic and bay leaves and cook for another 30 seconds, stirring frequently.

› Deglaze the pot with the beer, scraping the bottom with a wooden spoon until all the browned bits are

released. Stir constantly until it returns to a simmer. Add the stock and continue stirring until it returns to a simmer. Add the remaining 1 teaspoon salt and 1 teaspoon black pepper and the cayenne. Add the reserved chicken thighs (skin, bones, everything) and their fat and the sausage. Bring back to a bare simmer, being careful not to let it boil and not to let the roux scorch, reduce the heat to the lowest setting on your stove, and cover. Simmer for 3 hours, stirring every 30 minutes, scraping the bottom each time. Your gumbo should begin to thicken, but not like gravy. If it starts getting too thick before the 3 hours are up and you have to hit it with a little water to thin it, do so.

› Do *not* skim that fat off the top.

› Serve with rice. I put the gumbo down in each bowl first and then put the rice on top. Garnish with sliced green onions. If you want to bump up the heat, add a little scoop of pepper paste.

RULES OF GUMBO

Out there in the world, you may see shrimp gumbo with sausage in it. That's almost unheard of where I come from. Sea and land don't mix. We're not being prissy: If you put shrimp and sausage together, all you taste is sausage, and that's a waste of good shrimp. I see people breaking tradition and that's fine. I even do it myself from time to time. But land and sea just don't go together in gumbo.

THE TOUPS BURGER

This is the burger to end all burgers. It's got the perfect balance of fat and acid to make your mouth do the happy dance: bacon, cheese, squash pickles, and Creole aioli. Its intense meaty flavor comes from using high-quality brisket and adding delicious pork fat. To do it right, grind the meat yourself or ask a butcher to do it for you. This isn't where you want to buy meat that's preground and already wrapped up. | *Makes 6 (½-pound) burgers*

3½ pounds beef brisket, trimmed of all fat and finely ground

½ pound pork belly (use only the fatty end, not the meaty end), skin removed and finely ground

Grapeseed oil

Kosher salt

Burger Seasoning (recipe follows)

Creole Mustard Aioli (page 19)

6 large hamburger buns

12 ounces aged cheddar cheese, grated

12 slices bacon, cooked until crispy and broken in half

Squash Pickles (page 138)

> In a large bowl, mix together the cold ground brisket and cold fat by hand, like you would bread dough, folding over three or four times, until just combined. Do not overwork the mixture or you'll emulsify that fat and make it more like sausage.

> Divide the meat and fat mixture into six ½-pound patties. You want to shape your patties based on the size of your buns—I like the meat to hang over the bun a little bit, so I make a 5-inch patty for a 4-inch bun. Form the mixture into the patties, and press your thumb gently into the center of each. The negative space of your thumbprint will ensure the burger will cook flat, rather than puffed up like a football. Put the patties on a plate, cover, and chill in the fridge for at least 20 minutes, or up to a day.

> When you're ready to cook, heat a griddle or large cast iron skillet over medium-high heat. You want it hot and ready to go. I prefer a pan's flat surface because a hard sear on 100 percent of the meat makes a better burger; a grill will only get you grill marks. Once the skillet is hot, add enough oil to coat the bottom of the pan, about 1 tablespoon.

> Pull the patties out of the fridge and give them a generous coating of salt and burger seasoning on each side, about 1½ tablespoons of seasoning per patty. You want to form a crust with the seasoning.

> Place the patties in the pan, don't crowd them. Depending on the size of your griddle or skillet, you might have to cook them in batches. Sear the burgers hard over medium-high heat, 2 minutes on each side. Continue cooking until internal temperature is 130°F for a burger done to medium.

> While burgers are searing, toast your buns. Once the burgers are cooked, transfer them to a wire rack to rest for 1 minute.

> Assemble the burger, building it from the bottom up: Spread the bottom bun with aioli, add the patty, sprinkle with 2 ounces of grated cheddar cheese. On top of that, layer four half-slices of crispy bacon. Top the bacon with one full layer of overlapping pickle. When you look down, you want to see only pickle, not burger peeking through. Crown the whole thing with the aioli-smeared top bun. Now that's a damn burger.

BURGER SEASONING

¼ cup ground black pepper

¼ cup ground Aleppo pepper
(or paprika or crushed red
pepper flakes)

¼ cup ground arbol chile

› Whisk all the spices together in a small bowl. Keep in an airtight container until needed.

BROTHER BATTLES

One night at Christmas, when Mama and Daddy still lived at the old house in Rayne, we were driving around the property in a truck. Amanda and my brother Nathaniel were in the cab, and Daddy and I were in the back trying to shoot rabbits around the yard. Not just trying—we did shoot some.

Amanda got worn out with our jackassery and went to bed. A little while later I went to wake her up and said, "Baby, don't worry. Everything is fine. But I threw a rake at Nathaniel's face and he's bleeding real bad, so we're taking him to the dental office." Not the emergency room. Dad's dental office. We called my older brother Jason, also a dentist, to get us because he had slept off his Crown Royal buzz. And Jason sat there and sewed Nathaniel's face up, right there in the dental chair.

Nate's still got the scar—it's a T. The Toups brand. Yeah, I could have killed my little brother, or taken his eye out. But he threw a shovel at me, so I threw a rake at him. I nailed him from 30 yards, like I was King Leonidas with a javelin. I felt pretty bad, mostly because my mom shamed me. But it was a damn good shot.

CHICKEN LIVER MOUSSE

Why is this so good? It's mostly fat! A premium European-style butter is the key to nailing this recipe. Traditionally a chicken liver mousse calls for brandy and port. But I drink bourbon, not brandy, so I use bourbon and port instead. The pro move is to dip freshly made cracklins (page 32) into this. Holy shit. | *Serves 8 to 10*

- 1 pound chicken livers, cleaned of any blemishes (no bile spots or any little yellow spots)
- ¼ cup bourbon
- ¼ cup ruby port (not tawny)
- 1 tablespoon sugar

- 1 teaspoon kosher salt
- ½ teaspoon white pepper
- ⅛ teaspoon curing salt (optional, to preserve the color of the mousse)
- 1 tablespoon grapeseed oil

- ¾ cup (6 ounces) softened cream cheese
- ¾ cup (6 ounces) European-style unsalted butter (like Plugrá), softened to slightly warmer than room temperature
- Cane Syrup Gastrique (page 61), optional

› In a bowl, mix the chicken livers, bourbon, port, sugar, salt, white pepper, and curing salt (if using). Toss to mix well.

› Heat a large skillet (large enough to fit all the chicken livers in a single layer), over medium-high heat for a few minutes, then add the oil. Heat the oil until just shimmering—right before it begins to smoke. You want the skillet hot before adding the livers, so any liquid evaporates as soon as it hits the skillet. Add the chicken liver mixture to the skillet. Stirring constantly, cook the livers for about 5 to 10 minutes, until medium (or 135°F internal temperature). The centers should be pink, not red, and soft, but not slippery. It's better to undercook the livers than overcook them for this mousse.

› Transfer the livers and any juice in the skillet to a baking dish and arrange in a single layer. Chill the livers in the fridge for about an hour, until cool but not cold (50 to 60°F internal temperature).

› In a food processor, add the livers and their juices. (You should have about ¼ cup pan juices; if you don't, add water until you reach ¼ cup.) Add the cream cheese and butter. Pulse for about 10 seconds. Scrape the sides, then pulse for another 10 seconds. The liver mixture should be smooth with only a few small chunks. Taste and add salt as needed.

› Transfer the mousse to an airtight container and refrigerate until it's completely chilled and ready to serve.

› Using spoons, form quenelles of the mousse to serve. (If you prefer, you can put the mousse into individual serving ramekins straight from the food processor and cover with plastic wrap, making sure the plastic wrap is flush with the mousse to prevent any air from touching it.) I like to garnish with a drizzle of Cane Syrup Gastrique because I'm a fatass and love to add flavor everywhere.

CONFIT CHICKEN THIGHS

Confiting is a huge part of Cajun cooking. When my parents were little, they would pour hot fat over sausages to preserve them through the winter. We don't have cellars down here, so sometimes they'd just stick them under the house.

You can eat these immediately, but if you want the best chicken confit, make it a week beforehand and keep the thighs covered in the fridge, stored under the airtight blanket of lard. That extra time helps develop all this flavor that's just like "HELL YEAH!" | *Serves 4*

2 pounds (about 4) bone-in, skin-on chicken thighs

1 tablespoon kosher salt

2 teaspoons finely ground black pepper

8 cloves garlic, minced

1 tablespoon fresh thyme leaves, finely chopped

1 tablespoon fresh oregano leaves, finely chopped

1 tablespoon fresh rosemary leaves, finely chopped

1 quart (4 cups) rendered lard, or plain-Jane vegetable oil

Lacquered Collards (page 129), for serving

Note: You need to cure the thighs for a full 24 hours before you can cook them.

THE DAY BEFORE

› Season the thighs with all of the salt, using your fingers to rub the salt into the skin. Then season with the black pepper. In a small bowl, stir together the garlic, thyme, oregano, and rosemary and cake that onto the thighs. It's not going to want to stick on very well, so just kind of pack it on with your hands. Place the chicken thighs in a 9 x 9-inch baking dish, skin side up. Cram them in there in a single layer. Cover with plastic wrap and place in fridge. Let sit for 24 hours.

THE DAY OF

› Preheat the oven to 350°F.

› Remove the chicken thighs from the fridge. Pour the rendered lard over the thighs in the baking dish until they are almost fully covered with some of the skin still sticking out on top. You may not need all the lard.

› Cover the baking dish with aluminum foil and bake for 2½ hours, until the chicken skin is nice and crispy and the thighs are cooked through. Even with all of the lard, this dish is surprisingly not greasy.

› Remove the thighs from the baking dish and serve with the collards.

CONFIT CHICKEN HEARTS

This dish is so damn easy, and it's turned many people on to eating chicken hearts. People hear "hearts" and get weirded out, but the heart is just a muscle—it's meaty, not like offal—and is the least intimidating of all the organs if you just give it a chance. It tastes like dark meat chicken but with richer flavor. Hear me: *Chicken hearts taste like chicken.* Plus, if you're eating the chicken's heart, you're also tasting its delicious, delicious soul. | *Serves 8 to 10*

1 pound chicken hearts

2 teaspoons kosher salt

1 teaspoon ground black pepper

1 teaspoon smoked paprika

1 quart rendered lard, or plain-Jane vegetable oil

Note: Sometimes gizzards are easier to find than hearts, and you can substitute them instead. Use the same technique but cook them for 3 hours instead of 2.

› Preheat the oven to 350°F.

› In a medium bowl, toss the chicken hearts with the salt, black pepper, and smoked paprika and let them mingle for 30 minutes at room temperature. Place the hearts in a deep oven-proof baking vessel (I like to do it in a Dutch oven; I always use a bigger container than I need when I'm handling hot stuff). Pour the rendered lard over the hearts.

› Cover and bake for 2 hours. When they come out of the oven you are going to have boiling oil on your hands, so handle carefully.

› Remove the hearts from the oil with a slotted spoon and serve. They are great on a cracker with some mustard as a canapé. They're great as a Cajun shish kebab or to top a salad. I'm so down with a chicken heart salad.

› Alternately, you can make the hearts up to a week ahead of time. If you do them in advance, once they have cooked, leave them in the oil to store them. Let the oil cool to room temp and then put the whole Dutch oven, lid on, in the fridge. To serve, heat the Dutch oven in a 350°F oven or on top of the stove over low heat until the fat has melted and you can scoop the hearts from the oil, about 15 minutes. You can heat up the entire batch or just scoop out the amount you want to serve and bring those back up to temperature.

LUGE CANOE
ROASTED BONE MARROW

Our general manager at the Meatery got us doing the bone marrow luge: You drink a shot of whiskey straight through a leftover marrow bone. The alcohol strips the last of the marrow off the bone to give you a meaty, fatty shot of bourbon. It aids digestion for sure. Whoever gets the first shot definitely gets the best shot. But if you want to drink bourbon through a bone luge, you have to cook bone marrow first. | *Serves 2*

- 12 Confit Chicken Hearts (page 116), optional
- ½ beef femur, split in half lengthwise in a "canoe cut" (your butcher will either love you or hate you for this)
- 1 teaspoon kosher salt, divided
- 1 teaspoon ground black pepper, divided
- 1 teaspoon grapeseed oil
- 1½ teaspoons minced garlic
- ¼ cup bourbon
- 2 cups veal stock (page 13 or store-bought), reduced to ¼ cup
- 1 tablespoon unsalted butter
- 1 tablespoon chopped green onion (optional)
- Chicken Liver Mousse (page 113) and crostini, for serving (optional)

› Prepare the Confit Chicken Hearts, if using, up to a week ahead of time.

› Preheat the oven to 400°F.

› Season the bone marrow with ½ teaspoon of the salt and ½ teaspoon of the pepper. Place on a rimmed baking sheet, split side up, and roast for 12 minutes, or until an instant-read thermometer inserted into the middle of the bone marrow reads 155°F.

› While the marrow is roasting, heat a large skillet on low. Add the oil and swirl the pan to coat. Add the garlic and chicken hearts, if using, and cook, stirring occasionally, until it starts to toast and turns light brown. Don't let the pan get too hot. Burnt garlic is *no bueno.*

› Add the bourbon to deglaze the pan and get the fuck back. Fireball! As soon as the alcohol has flamed off, add the reduced veal stock. Stir in the remaining ½ teaspoon each salt and pepper. Remove the pan from heat and stir in the butter.

› Remove the roasted bone marrow from the oven and transfer to a serving plate. Pour the sauce over it. No part of the face of the bone (cut bone marrow side) should be naked. Top with chopped green onion if you like. Serve. As a true baller move, serve the marrow alongside crostini topped with chicken liver mousse.

› Once you've eaten the marrow, cover your face to hide your shame from God. Then drink a whiskey shot through the bone luge. Make sure you put in enough whiskey. I think ¼ cup is the right amount.

PARMESAN-BRAISED TRIPE

I developed this dish because I needed a way to use leftover Parmesan rinds. I'd heard of people putting them in braises to get more flavor, so I thought I'd try it with tripe. And it's incredible. Now, whenever I have a bunch of Parmesan rinds, it's an excuse to buy tripe.

I let this cook overnight because it takes that long to break down the tripe. Undercooked tripe is disgusting—it tastes like rubber bands. By cooking the tripe for so long, it comes out tender but not falling apart. The Parmesan rinds add deep and wonderful umami. The tomato brings the acid. I slather this on bread, but it also makes a really good pasta sauce. | *Makes 6 to 8 hearty servings*

10 cups chicken stock (page 12 or store-bought)

1½ cups (two 6-ounce cans) tomato paste

6 ounces Parmesan rinds (or Parmesan, but the rinds are better)

8 pounds tripe, cut into 1-inch squares

1 cup balsamic vinegar

1 tablespoon crushed red pepper flakes

1 tablespoon kosher salt

1 teaspoon ground black pepper

Crostini or French bread, for serving

EQUIPMENT
Cheesecloth

Butcher twine

› Preheat the oven to 225°F. In a medium saucepot, bring the stock to a simmer over medium heat. Once it's simmering, whisk in the tomato paste until fully dissolved.

› Make a package of all the Parmesan rinds with a piece of cheesecloth and tie the bundle with butcher twine.

› Take a piece of parchment paper and cut it to the diameter of your large Dutch oven (or large high-sided roasting pan).

› Put the tripe in the Dutch oven or roasting pan. Add the stock-tomato mixture, balsamic vinegar, pepper flakes, salt, and pepper and stir to incorporate all ingredients well. Add the cheesecloth-wrapped Parmesan rinds. Place the cut parchment paper on top of the mixture in the Dutch oven. (The parchment helps keep the tripe from drying out as it cooks.) Put the lid on the dish (or cover tightly with aluminum foil) and bake for 13 hours. Yes, 13 hours.

› Pull it out of the oven and discard the parchment paper. The tripe should be the consistency of a thick tomato sauce—thick enough to spread, not soupy, but not like tomato paste either. Remove the cheesecloth sachet of Parmesan rinds and give it a good squeeze over the pot with a pair of tongs—there's a lot of good juice up in there—then discard the sachet. Give the tripe mixture a stir, and it's ready to serve.

› Serve in a bowl with buttered crostini or French bread for dipping.

ROASTED VEGETABLES
IN A BACON, SHERRY, AND MAYONNAISE VINAIGRETTE

I can figure out a way to work mayonnaise or aioli into anything. For this dish, I roast vegetables hard in bacon grease, until I near about burn them. Then I toss in crisped bacon, a big squeeze of Blue Plate mayonnaise, and a squirt of sherry vinegar. It creams up and is fucking killer. It's one of my wife's favorite things that I do—and I have my share of bedroom tricks. | *Serves 4*

6 slices thick-cut bacon	2 tablespoons mayonnaise	Pinch ground dried piri piri chile (optional)
1 head cauliflower, cut into florets	½ tablespoon aged sherry vinegar	
1 poblano pepper, finely diced	2 teaspoons kosher salt	

Note: I like cauliflower for this, but you can substitute any vegetable, such as a couple crowns of broccoli or a couple pounds of Brussels sprouts.

› Preheat the oven to 400°F. Place the bacon slices on a rimmed baking sheet and cook in the oven for about 20 minutes, until the bacon is crispy. Remove the bacon and reserve the baking sheet with the rendered fat. Crumble or roughly chop the bacon and set aside.

› Add the cauliflower florets and poblano pepper to the baking sheet and toss in the grease. Place back in the oven and roast for 45 minutes, or until the vegetables have a nice toasty char.

› To the roasted vegetables on the sheet, add the crumbled bacon, mayonnaise, vinegar, salt, and piri piri pepper, if using. Gently toss everything together until the vegetables are well covered. Serve.

GRILLED GARDEN VEGETABLES
WITH BACON VINAIGRETTE

Want to make your vegetables taste better and have your friends love you? Char the hell out of some on the grill and then toss them in a bacon vinaigrette. These are vegetables so unhealthy a Cajun might actually eat them.

You can do this dish year-round with whatever is in season: eggplant and zucchini, radishes, green beans, radicchio, or others. If the vegetable is sliceable, slice it. If it's broccoli or cauliflower, cut into quarter-size florets; if green beans, leave them whole. | *Serves 4*

8 slices thick-cut bacon

5 cloves garlic, peeled

3 anchovy filets

½ cup apple cider vinegar

½ cup canola oil

1 pound assorted vegetables, cut into ¼-inch slices

1½ teaspoons kosher salt

1 teaspoon ground black pepper

½ teaspoon crushed red pepper flakes

1 tablespoon extra virgin olive oil

› Preheat the grill to high (about 500°F). Preheat the oven to 400°F.

› Place the bacon slices on a rimmed baking sheet and cook in the oven for about 20 minutes, until the bacon is crispy. Remove the bacon and reserve the baking sheet with the rendered fat. Crumble the bacon and set aside.

› In a blender, combine the garlic, anchovies, and vinegar and put the lid on. Turn the blender on and slowly drizzle in the canola oil. This is never going to be a fully emulsified vinaigrette, so don't fret if it looks like it's breaking. Add the reserved bacon fat (about 1½ tablespoons, but if you have more from cooking your bacon, just toss it all in) and keep the blender buzzing for 5 seconds to combine all the ingredients. Keep warm. I like to put it in a metal container, like a mixing bowl, and keep it by the grill while I cook the vegetables. The vinaigrette doesn't need to be hot, just not too cold because the bacon fat will congeal if you let it.

› In a large bowl or on a rimmed baking sheet, toss the vegetables with the salt, pepper, pepper flakes, and olive oil. Place the vegetables on the hot grill in a single layer and cook on each side for about 2 minutes. They should char on the outside while keeping the crunch or snap of fresh crudités. They should be really crispy and charred, not all wimpy and overcooked; high heat is key here. Remove the vegetables from the grill and put in a nonreactive bowl.

› Toss the grilled vegetables in the bacon vinaigrette. Top with the crumbled bacon. Serve.

BRENT'S BRAISED MULTI-GREENS

If you like to measure, this recipe will drive you crazy. This is my dad's recipe for braised greens and he throws in however much will fit in his 3-gallon pot—approximately 3 pounds. Basically, just get yourself a shitload of greens and go to town. Choose any combination of greens you like. The ones listed below are what Daddy grows, so that's what we eat. You can't do this wrong. I promise. | *Serves 6*

2 tablespoons neutral vegetable oil, like canola or grapeseed

½ pound andouille sausage, finely chopped

1 small onion, finely diced

3 pounds assorted greens, like kale, purple mustard greens, mustard greens, curly mustard greens, and collards

2 cups water

2 tablespoons sugar

1 tablespoon kosher salt

› Heat the oil in a 3-gallon pot over medium heat. Add the andouille and onion and cook until the fat is rendered from the sausage and it's nicely browned, about 15 minutes. Pack the whole green leaves into the pot, as many as you can fit. As they start cooking down, cut the greens with kitchen shears directly in the pot to help break them down some more. Add the water, sugar, and salt and bring to a boil. Cover, reduce the heat to low, and simmer until the greens are tender, about 30 minutes.

ANDOUILLE

Andouille is the quintessential Cajun sausage. It's packed with cayenne, garlic, smoked paprika, and black, red, and white pepper, and it's typically smoked. It's the nicest and coolest of all the sausages, but it's rarely eaten on its own—andouille is mostly used as an ingredient in other dishes, like gumbo.

Normally sausage is made up with leftover bits—fat and off-cuts—that are ground up with spices to make sure nothing goes to waste. Andouille is actually made with the choice cuts, so you end up with big chunks of meat in the sausage. You might have hand-diced chunks of loin meat tucked in there, a sort of meat marbling. It's like a Cajun way of showing off: "Look how nice my sausage is," said in the only nonsexual way that sentence could ever be uttered.

LACQUERED COLLARDS

I also call these braised or sticky collards. I put a full pound of meat in the greens: My preference is for equal amounts brisket and bacon, to get that smoked barbecue flavor from the brisket and the fatty goodness from the bacon. But if you have some leftover sausage to throw in, that would be cool too. Leftover piece of pork roast? Sure. What you use doesn't matter as long as you have a full pound of meat. That's what makes the collards so good. They go great with any pork or chicken dish, and are the best collards around. They may not be too healthy, but you didn't pop open this book for that. | *Serves 6 to 8*

- 1 tablespoon neutral vegetable oil, like canola or grapeseed
- 1 large onion, thinly sliced
- 10 cloves garlic, peeled and crushed
- ½ pound bacon, cut into ¼-inch dice
- ½ pound brisket (cooked), cut into ¼-inch dice
- 1 (12-ounce) bottle dark beer (porter or stout)
- 2 cups chicken stock (page 12 or store-bought)
- ¼ cup cane syrup
- 2 teaspoons kosher salt
- ½ teaspoon ground black pepper
- ½ teaspoon cayenne pepper
- 2 (1-pound) bunches collard greens, stemmed and torn into pieces about the size of a dollar bill, then cut in half lengthwise

› Heat a large stockpot or Dutch oven over medium-high heat for a couple of minutes. Add the oil and heat until shimmering, about 1 minute. Add the onion and cook for 4 to 6 minutes, stirring occasionally, until it starts to brown. You want good caramelization on the onion. Add the crushed garlic and cook for 1 minute, stirring occasionally. Add the bacon and brisket and cook for 1 minute, stirring occasionally, until the fat begins to render.

› Add the beer, stock, cane syrup, salt, black pepper, and cayenne. Give it a good stir. Reduce the heat to medium and bring mixture up to a simmer. Add one-third of collard greens and stir. Cover the pot and cook for 10 minutes. Add another third of the collards,

stir, cover, and cook for 10 more minutes. Add the last third of collards, stir, and cover. Cook for 45 minutes over medium heat. (We're intentionally cooking pretty hot because there's a lot of liquid in the pot and you're ultimately steaming the collards to break them down.)

› Uncover the pot and give it a good stir. Reduce the heat to medium-low, keeping at a low simmer, and cook uncovered for 1½ hours, stirring every 10 minutes. Stir them often because you want the syrup and stock to really adhere to all of the greens—really lacquer them. There won't be a lot of water left at the bottom of the pot when these are done, only about a cup of liquid total. They'll be sticky and meaty and incredible.

SWEET & SOUR ROASTED BRUSSELS SPROUTS

The sweet and sour sauce goes well not only with Brussels sprouts but other vegetables: broccoli, cauliflower, carrots, butternut squash, green beans—anything you can roast in a pan. It's a sauce that fires on every cylinder in your mouth: It's sweet and sour, but also spicy, salty, gingery, and savory. I've even played with it as seasoning for beef tartare. | *Serves 4*

- 1 pound Brussels sprouts (if small, leave whole; if large, halve or quarter them into 1-inch chunks)
- 1 tablespoon extra virgin olive oil
- ½ teaspoon kosher salt
- ½ teaspoon ground black pepper
- Sweet & Sour Sauce (recipe below)

› Preheat the oven to 400°F. Toss the Brussels sprouts, oil, salt, and pepper in a mixing bowl to season. Arrange in a baking sheet large enough for the sprouts to fit in a single layer. Roast for 20 minutes, until nicely charred.

Let cool on baking sheet for 2 minutes. Transfer sprouts to a mixing bowl, drizzle with 2 tablespoons sauce, and toss until Brussels sprouts are well coated.

SWEET & SOUR SAUCE
Makes 1 cup

- ½ cup soy sauce
- ½ cup aged sherry vinegar
- ½ cup cane syrup (or dark molasses)
- ½ teaspoon crushed red pepper flakes
- 10 cloves garlic, minced
- ¼ cup (2 ounces) minced fresh ginger

› Heat all the ingredients in a small saucepan over medium heat until simmering. Reduce the heat to low and maintain a simmer for 55 minutes, swirling the pan every 5 minutes, until the liquid reduces to about 1 cup. As it reduces, there will be sugar on the rim that will start to char, so swirling will take that sugar back into the liquid. This will burn if you look at it wrong because of all the sugar, so the swirling is important.

› The shelf life on this sauce is longer than human civilization. It's got so much salt and vinegar in it, you could drop a raw fish in it and it would be fine. It's basically a preservative at this point. What I'm saying: You can make giant batches and it will keep for a looooooong time. So do it.

MAW MAW TOUPS'
ROUX PEAS

I used to think instant roux was evil, but I've come around. If you want to cook some Cajun food and you just don't have a lot of time, it's not a bad idea. Yes, I even keep some instant roux at home. And quite frankly, it's perfect for making a little batch of roux peas. So yes, use instant roux here. And use canned peas. It's a straight-up home cheat that even a Cajun grandmother would say is okay. I know. Because mine literally did. | *Serves 4*

- 2 tablespoons unsalted butter
- 1 bunch green onions, chopped, green and white parts separated
- 8 ounces mushrooms, quartered, with stems
- 1 (15-ounce) can small green peas (I prefer no. 1 sieve petit pois from Dubon or very young small sweet peas from Le Sueur), drained
- 1 cup cold chicken stock (page 12 or store-bought)
- 1 tablespoon instant dark roux
- 1 teaspoon kosher salt
- ½ teaspoon ground black pepper
- ¼ teaspoon cayenne pepper

› In a medium saucepot, clarify the butter over medium-low heat. Add the whites of the green onions and sweat for 1 minute. Stir in the mushrooms and cook for 7 minutes, until they have a little color on them. Add the peas and stock. Stir in the instant roux, salt, black pepper, and cayenne. Bring to a simmer and cook for about 20 minutes, uncovered. When the liquid has the consistency of a thick gravy, stir in the green onion greens. Serve.

› You can eat these peas by themselves, over rice, over mashed potatoes, as the gravy over chicken fried steak. You can even poach eggs in them.

HOMETOWN PRIDE

My hometown is the frog capital of the world, home of the Rayne Frog Festival. Every little town around here has a festival. I think by the time they got to Rayne, they'd near run out of festivals. Breaux Bridge has crawfish; Crowley has rice. They got to Rayne, and it was like, "You can have frogs or skunks." Okay, we'll take the frogs.

ISAAC'S CORNBREAD

There is an argument in the South about whether you should put sugar in cornbread. Well, growing up, we had Jiffy cornbread, and it's sweet. I'm a fat boy. I like my sugar. So I say put it in. And I think sweet and savory are gold. Candied pork belly, cane syrup gastrique on a pork chop (page 61), sweet pickled fennel (page 141) on lamb neck (page 62). I'm not very good at desserts, but I'm really good at sugary savory, and having a little sugar in my cornbread helps me achieve that. | *Makes 1 skillet*

4 large eggs	2 cups yellow cornmeal	1 tablespoon baking powder
1¼ cups cold whole milk	2 cups all-purpose flour	½ teaspoon kosher salt
¼ cup honey	1¼ cups sugar	½ pound (2 sticks) unsalted butter, melted

Note: I'll say it till my jaw falls off: Whisk your dry ingredients. Powders act more like liquids than solids when mixing them together. By using a whisk you can fully combine them, which is especially helpful when you're baking.

› Preheat the oven to 350°F. Place a 12-inch cast iron skillet in the oven to heat up as the oven heats.

› Whisk the eggs, milk, and honey together in a small bowl. In a separate large bowl, whisk together the cornmeal, flour, sugar, baking powder, and salt. Pour the egg-milk mixture into the dry ingredients and whisk vigorously for 8 seconds, just until all your flour is moistened. If it's slightly lumpy, that's okay. I'd rather it be lumpy than overworked. Overworking will give you dense cornbread. Add the melted butter and immediately mix vigorously with the whisk for another 4 or 5 seconds.

› Remove the hot skillet from the oven and pour in the batter. Place back in oven and bake for 30 to 40 minutes, until a cake tester comes out clean.

› Serve with room temperature butter and cane syrup. (Or use it to make Crawfish Cornbread Dressing, page 88.)

HORSERADISH DEVILED EGGS

There's enough horseradish in here to make the hair stand up on the back of your neck. These aren't your grandmother's deviled eggs. Or if they are, I'd really like to share rodeo drinking stories with her. | *Makes 18 to 20*

10 hard-boiled large eggs, peeled and halved, yolks and whites separated

¼ cup mayonnaise

2 anchovy filets, smashed and minced

3 tablespoons prepared horseradish (hot)

½ teaspoon ground Aleppo pepper (or paprika or crushed red pepper flakes)

2 teaspoons kosher salt, divided

½ teaspoon ground black pepper

1 teaspoon hot sauce

1 teaspoon Worcestershire sauce

Pickled Jalapeños (page 139) or Isaac's Pepper Paste of Pain (page 21), for serving

› Place the egg yolks, mayonnaise, anchovies, horseradish, Aleppo pepper, 1 teaspoon of the salt, and the black pepper in a food processor. Combine on high for 10 seconds, until smooth.

› In a large mixing bowl, combine the remaining 1 teaspoon salt, the hot sauce, and Worcestershire. Place the egg whites in this mixture and gently toss with your hands to season. Tradition says not to season the egg whites of a deviled egg. But why the hell not? But the whites are fragile, so handle them like you'd handle yourself if a mosquito landed on your genitals—very carefully.

› Place 2 tablespoons of the filling into each egg white half. I use a piping bag (or a ziplock bag with the corner cut off) to make it look fancy, but you can just use a spoon. There is really only enough filling to fill 18 egg white halves. Before you get mad at me for under-delivering on filling, know that it is damn near impossible to get all 20 halves peeled and seasoned intact, so I've created this recipe to make sure you get 18 really great, well-filled deviled eggs. Nothing pisses me off like a piddly deviled egg with just a little bit of filling. If you want to stretch it to more eggs, that's on you.

› Garnish each egg with a slice of pickled jalapeño slice or ¼ teaspoon pepper paste. Squares of crispy bacon also go well on these. Trout roe is also another one of my favorite toppers.

SQUASH PICKLES

When I make pickles, I basically follow the idea that half of the recipe is liquid. Of that liquid, half is water and half is vinegar (plus a little extra for a flavor boost). It's my rule of thumb for playing around with all sorts of pickles. You can change the spices and flavors however you want, as long as you keep the basic ratio the same. | *Makes 1 quart*

4 cups ⅛-inch-thick rounds of yellow squash, zucchini, or a combination

1¼ cups white wine vinegar (or white balsamic vinegar)

1 cup water

¼ cup sugar

1 teaspoon kosher salt

½ teaspoon curry powder

½ teaspoon crushed red pepper flakes (optional)

› Pack the sliced squash in a food-safe container, like a 1-quart Mason jar.

› In a saucepan set over high heat, combine the vinegar, water, sugar, salt, curry powder, and pepper flakes (if using). Stir one good time when you put everything in the pot, and then leave it alone as the liquid comes to a boil. After it has boiled, pour the hot liquid over the squash. Let it cool down to room temperature, cover, and refrigerate. These will keep refrigerated and tightly covered for up to 2 weeks.

PICKLED JALAPEÑOS

I garnish with pickled jalapeños a lot. Sometimes I use the pickling liquid to season other dishes. The pickle juice is really good for pickleback shots (a shot of whiskey chased with a shot of pickling liquid). In other words, I always keep these on hand. They work in small or large format batches, from a quart up to a gallon—just double or quadruple the recipe. | *Makes 1 quart*

- 1 quart (about 25) jalapeños, sliced into ⅛-inch-thick slices
- 5½ cups ice-cold water, divided
- 1½ cups white wine vinegar
- ½ cup sugar
- 2 tablespoons honey
- ¼ teaspoon kosher salt
- 1 teaspoon ground black pepper
- 1 bay leaf

› Put the jalapeños in 5 cups of ice-cold water. Agitate gently and skim off any seeds that come to the top. There will be some seeds left on the slices, and that's okay. Drain well.

› Combine the remaining ½ cup cold water, the vinegar, sugar, honey, salt, pepper, and bay leaf in a large saucepan. Bring to a boil, reduce the heat, and simmer for 20 minutes uncovered. Add the jalapeños to a 1-quart Mason jar or other container and pour the hot liquid over them. Let sit out until cooled to room temperature, then cover and refrigerate. These will keep refrigerated for a few weeks.

PICKLED FENNEL

I love fennel or anise flavors. I quadruple down on that flavor here by combining fresh fennel, Herbsaint, fennel seed, and anise seed. This pickle goes well with any fatty meats or sausages, but I think it's best with my Braised Lamb Neck (page 62). | *Makes 2 quarts*

8 cups thinly sliced fennel (about 5 bulbs)

3 tablespoons fennel seed, toasted

1 tablespoon coriander seed

1 tablespoon anise seed

2 cups rice wine vinegar

2 cups water

½ cup Herbsaint

½ cup sugar

› Divide the sliced fennel, fennel seed, coriander seed, and anise seed evenly between two 1-quart Mason jars.

› In a 4-quart saucepan over high heat, bring the vinegar, water, Herbsaint, and sugar to a boil, stir, and reduce to a simmer. Simmer for 10 minutes.

› Pour the hot liquid into the Mason jars over the fennel and spices, dividing equally. Stir well. Let cool to room temperature. Cover and refrigerate for 24 hours. The pickled fennel will keep in the refrigerator for a couple of weeks.

PICKLED GRILLED PINEAPPLE

I will try and pickle everything I can get my hands on. And, as you may have noticed, I love to char the crap out of stuff. This recipe is the combination of both of those proclivities, and it's maybe my favorite pickle I've ever created. Next time you fix a gin and soda, throw one of these in. It goes great with my Chile-Marinated Crab Claws (page 179). And it's outstanding with every sausage I can imagine. If you're one of those freaks who likes to put pineapple on pizza . . . I love you. | *Makes 2 quarts*

3 whole ripe pineapples, peeled, cut top to bottom into long quarters, and core removed

1½ quarts white wine vinegar

5 cups water

1 pound dark brown sugar

1 cup granulated sugar

1 teaspoon crushed red pepper flakes

› Heat the grill to high (about 500°F). Grill the pineapple slabs for 1 to 2 minutes on each side, until nicely charred. Once the pineapple is cool enough to handle, cut it into roughly 1-inch dice and divide evenly between two 1-quart Mason jars.

› Combine the vinegar, water, both sugars, and pepper flakes in a medium saucepan. Bring to a simmer over medium-high heat and stir to make sure all the sugar is dissolved. Once simmering, reduce the heat to low and cook uncovered for 20 minutes.

› Pour the hot liquid over the pineapple into the jars, dividing evenly. Let sit until cooled to room temperature, about an hour. Refrigerate until fully chilled, then cover tightly. These are ready to eat as soon as they are fully cold, but they taste better the next day. The refrigerated pickled pineapple will keep for a couple of weeks.

PICKLED QUAIL (OR CHICKEN) EGGS

Pickled eggs are a thing here because there are so many quail in the area. I love to pickle them because it makes for a quick, easy snack. They have more flavor than a normal chicken egg, with a deeper darker yolk. And the small size means they pickle faster. These little eggs have a wonderful pepper flavor that isn't too hot.

This makes a large batch, but there's no sense in doing this for a small number of quail eggs because they take so long to pickle (about a week) and are a pain in the ass to peel. You might as well knock out a whole bunch at once. | *Makes 4 dozen pickled quail eggs (or 1 dozen chicken eggs)*

4 dozen quail eggs

1½ cups cider vinegar

1 cup hot sauce

1 tablespoon whole yellow mustard seed

5 cloves garlic, minced

1 tablespoon kosher salt

1 teaspoon finely ground black pepper

3 bay leaves

Note: To make this recipe with chicken eggs, hard-boil and peel 1 dozen chicken eggs, then use two 1-quart Mason jars, triple the pickling brine recipe, and refrigerate for 2 weeks. Because they are so much larger, they need to sit in the pickling brine longer.

› In a stockpot, bring 3 quarts of water to a rolling boil. Gently add the quail eggs. I like to use a basket strainer that fits perfectly in the pot, so I put the quail eggs in the basket and then just lower the whole basket into the pot. If you don't have a basket strainer, you can use a mesh strainer—or just drop them carefully in the water. Boil for 1 minute. Remove the eggs from the boiling water. Empty the pot and fill with ice water. Submerge the eggs in the ice water to shock. Keep in ice water until completely cooled, about 10 minutes, adding more ice to keep it cold.

› Find some rube to peel all of these eggs. (Seriously, this step sucks.) Once all of the eggs are peeled, place carefully in a 1-quart Mason jar.

› Combine the vinegar, hot sauce, mustard, garlic, salt, pepper, and bay leaves in a small saucepan and bring to a boil. Once the liquid has boiled, remove from the heat and pour hot over the eggs. Let sit out for 1 hour, until cooled to room temperature. Refrigerate, uncovered for 4 hours, until the mixture is completely chilled through. Once chilled, tightly cover and refrigerate for 7 days. Every other day, turn it upside down and put the jar back in the fridge, alternating upside down and right side up. (All the good stuff settles at the bottom.)

› The eggs are ready to eat after 7 days—you could eat them earlier, but the flavor won't be near as good. They'll keep for several weeks in the refrigerator.

DOUBLE DILL PICKLES

This is the very first pickle I ever made growing up, me and my dad. I don't know if this is a recipe he made up or not. He'd say yes, he invented it. But I have no way of knowing if that's a lie. Cajuns have a funny way with the truth.

These spicy sweet dill pickles are good for burgers or served with charcuterie. They are even great right out of the damn jar while you stand at the open door of the refrigerator in your underwear. | *Makes 1 gallon*

1 (1-gallon) jar whole dill pickles (yes, like a store-bought jar of whole dill pickles)

1 pound brown sugar

2 tablespoons hot sauce

› Remove the pickles from brine. Reserve the brine and save the jar. These are going to go right back in there.

› Cut the pickles into ½-inch-thick slices and put back in the jar.

› In a large stockpot, combine the reserved brine, brown sugar, and hot sauce. Bring to a boil and stir. Once the sugar is fully dissolved, pour the hot liquid back over the pickles directly in the pickle jar. Let cool to room temperature. Refrigerate for 24 hours and they are good to go. They will keep refrigerated for several weeks.

THE TOUPS PALATE CLEANSER
(CUCUMBER SALAD WITH SHERRY-DIJON VINAIGRETTE)

When I was growing up, Daddy would slice whatever vegetables we had in the garden real thin and mix them with vinegar and soy sauce. In the summer, that was cucumbers, yellow squash, or tomatoes. In winter, radishes or turnips. He never called it a palate cleanser, but it was. It was something to eat between bites of all the other rich food on the table. This is a variation of his original. And if you're feeling frisky, crown it with a dollop of Blue Plate mayonnaise. Because why the hell not?

I peel my cucumbers like they're candy striped, using a bar zester to give a striped look before I slice them. At the house, Daddy would rough-peel them with a knife, so they looked a little ganked up. That's probably why I like to see a little skin on the cucumber. | *Serves 4*

Note: Salt leeches the cucumber water out and dilutes the dressing and can make it look soupy and weird. This is one dish you definitely can't make a day ahead.

- 1½ cups aged sherry vinegar
- 1½ cups soy sauce
- ¾ cup extra virgin olive oil
- ½ cup Dijon mustard
- 2 large cucumbers (any kind), peeled as you like
- ½ teaspoon kosher salt
- ½ teaspoon ground black pepper

› Combine the vinegar, soy sauce, olive oil, and mustard in a blender and blend well. You don't have to drizzle the oil separately because you're not emulsifying it with egg. The vinaigrette will keep refrigerated for weeks, and any leftovers (you'll have plenty) can be used to dress any vegetable, from tomatoes and squash to radishes and turnips, or as a salad dressing.

› Slice the cucumbers ⅛ inch thick and season with the salt and pepper. Dress with ¼ cup vinaigrette, or more to taste. Serve immediately.

Pickled Quail Eggs

• CAJUN GAMES •

SEVEN-CARD MEXICAN SWEAT

I have no clue why we call it Seven-Card Mexican Sweat. But everybody gets seven cards, face down. You never look at them. The dealer puts one card in the middle. The person to the left of the dealer has to flip his cards over until he beats the center card. Once they beat the center card, it goes to the next person. If you flip all seven and haven't beaten the person before you, you're done and the next person goes on. The winner is the last man standing.

Pickled Fennel

Pickled Grilled Pineapple

Pickled Watermelon Rind

Double Dill Pickles

Squash Pickles

Pickled Jalapeño

PICKLED WATERMELON RIND

This is a great summertime thing to go with anything smoked, spicy, charred, or grilled. It's a great palate cleanser. It goes great with a link of boudin. And because I juice the watermelon flesh to put in the pickling brine, this is the only pickled watermelon rind I've ever had that actually tastes like watermelon. | *Makes 1 gallon*

1 (15-pound) watermelon
   (about the size of a
   bowling ball)

1 cup sugar
4 cups apple cider vinegar

› With a peeler or sharp knife, remove the green skin (not the white rind) from the watermelon. I do this by cutting a thin disc off each end to make them flat, standing the watermelon on its end, and thinly slicing or peeling the skin off. Discard the peel.

› With a sharp knife, remove the rind in long strips, making sure you keep the rind free of watermelon meat as much as possible.

› Cut the rind into ¼-inch chunks. You're going to have some odd ends, and that's okay. You should have about a gallon of diced rind. Divide the rind among four 1-quart Mason jars and set aside.

› Take the meat of the watermelon and cut into 1-inch pieces. Don't worry about how pretty they are, because you're going to bust them up in the food processor.

› In small batches, run the watermelon meat through the processor for 45 seconds, or until completely smooth. You don't want any chunks here.

› Place a colander over a large bowl or food-safe bucket. Pour the pureed watermelon through the colander and collect the juice in the bowl. You're straining to remove large chunks (the fiber and roughage). Let the pureed watermelon sit in the colander for 30 minutes until all the juice runs out—you'll be left with a lot of pulp in the colander. You don't want to rush it or smash it through because that will force pulp into the juice. Once the juice has fully drained, discard the pulp.

› Put the watermelon juice in a 1-gallon pot over medium heat. Bring the juice up to a simmer (don't boil it hard because it can burn easily), and cook for about 45 minutes, until it reduces to 4 cups (1 quart) of syrupy liquid. While it's still over the heat, add the sugar and vinegar and stir. Bring it back up to a simmer until the sugar dissolves. Immediately remove from the heat and pour over the watermelon rind in the Mason jars.

› Let the liquid cool to room temperature for about an hour. Loosely place the cap on the top of the jar or loosely cover with plastic wrap; air should be able to escape. Place the jars in the fridge for 24 hours, then eat or screw the lids on tightly. They'll keep in the fridge for several weeks.

FENNEL MARMALADE

I've talked about doubling down on flavors—this marmalade uses fennel (the tops of the fennel bulb that are usually discarded), star anise, and Pernod to *triple* down on anise flavor. It packs a wallop. It eats like a sticky fennel relish or a rich caramelized onion marmalade. | *Makes 2 cups*

1 cup Pernod

1 cup sugar

2 tablespoons rice wine vinegar

4 pods star anise

Tops of 8 bulbs of fennel (no fronds, just the green stalks), finely diced

⅛ teaspoon kosher salt

› In a large cold sauté pan, add the Pernod. Heat on high until it starts to bubble. Push the Pernod right to edge of the pan and tip the pan toward the flame to ignite. (You can use a long-handled lighter instead.) Beware: Firestarter. This will make a *large* flame. Be aware of your surroundings. Once the Pernod ignites, turn the heat down to medium.

› Once the fire has died out, add the sugar, vinegar, and star anise. Stir over medium heat until the sugar has dissolved. Add the fennel tops and salt to that liquid and stir. Reduce heat to low. Cook, stirring every 5 minutes, for 40 minutes. Be sure to scrape the edges and bottom of the pan—because of the high sugar content, this will want to burn. By the end, almost all of the liquid should be gone, and it should look slightly golden brown. You'll have a wonderful fennel jam with a triple anise flavor that goes great with pâtés and chicken liver mousse, and rocks it on a cheese board.

HONEYSHINE

My daddy makes homemade wine that might best be described as an acquired taste. I've followed in his footsteps but learned a few things on my own to help it go down easier. With the help of a Christmas gift from Amanda—a small still and a cassette burner—I like to make honey wine (local honey, water, and yeast) and distill it into a moonshine that I sweeten with more honey. It's a real handmade country project, and quite frankly, it makes me feel like a badass. Look! I made stuff that you can light on fire!

I call it Dr. Calarat's Honeyshine. That name was made up by my father and one of his friends when they made wine. I loved it so much (the name, not their wine, let's be VERY clear) that I decided if I ever made alcohol, Dr. Calarat would be part of the name. The honey wine takes two weeks to ferment, a few hours to distill to honeyshine, and a flash to drink it.

SOUTHERN COMFORT PEACH JAM

This jam is perfect for when you've got excess peaches, like when you've gotten a deal or a neighbor was feeling generous. It goes great on cheese boards and with roasted game. We also put it on venison. But it also works well on a piece of Bunny white bread or in a PB&J. You can batch this recipe up to infinity. | *Makes 2 cups*

2 pounds medium-size, overripe peaches (about 10 peaches)	1 cup Southern Comfort (100-proof)	¼ teaspoon citric acid (or ½ teaspoon white wine vinegar)
	1 cup sugar	⅛ teaspoon kosher salt

Note: I like to use citric acid instead of lemon juice or another vinegar because I don't like to add any extra flavors to the peaches. If you've got a good ripe peach, you don't want to mess with that. So rather than adding lemon juice to add acid and flavor, I add citric acid because it has no flavor beyond its tartness.

› I like to just squeeze the peaches over a bowl to crush them. Grab a whole peach in your hand. Squeeze it over the bowl to get all the good stuff out until all you're left with is a pit—even the skin should be in the bowl, all crushed up. Imagine crushing the skulls of your enemies to get their brains. Repeat.

› Put this mixture in a food processor and blend for 1 minute, or until completely smooth (it won't hurt for it to go longer, you want everything pureed evenly). I like to include the skin because it adds balance from the tannins, much like you'd get from a nice glass of wine, and body. Once you puree it, you won't be able to tell it's skin, but it really helps temper all the sugar we're adding. Once it's all blended it will have the consistency of a peach smoothie—resist the urge to drink it.

› Put a large nonstick sauté pan over medium-low heat. Once the pan is hot, add the Southern Comfort and ignite the liquid. This will make a large flame—be warned. Continue to cook until the fire dies off, about 1 minute, then add the sugar, citric acid, salt, and peach puree. Give it a good stir with a heat-proof spatula. Keep the heat at medium-low and bring the mixture up to a simmer. Once the mixture is simmering, reduce the heat to the lowest possible setting. Cook for about 40 minutes, until the mixture reduces to 2 cups; stir with spatula every 5 minutes (stirring from edges toward the center to keep the edges clean as you reduce). This is high sugar, and it's going to want to burn, so keep that heat low. When it's ready, it will have a jam-like consistency.

› Transfer to any food-safe container that has a lid and let cool to room temperature. Cover and place in fridge, where it will keep for up to 2 weeks.

THE FISH CAMP

After a day fishing at a lake near his house, Boudreaux is walking
home carrying two big ol' fish in a bucket. He dun been approached
by the game warden, who asks for his fishing license. Naturally
Boudreaux ain't got none.

He says to the warden, "I didn't catch dese fishes, dey my pets. Every
day I come down to de lake and dey jump out de bucket and I let dem
swim for a while, an' when I whistles, dey jumps back in de bucket so
we can go home."

The warden, not believing him, says, "Now, you know it's illegal
to fish without a license."

Boudreaux, he turn to de warden and say, "If you don't believe me,
den watch," and throws the fish back in the water.

The warden say, "Now whistle to your fish and show me that
they will come back out."

Boudreaux, he turn back to de warden and say with a smile,
"What fish?"

Down in Grand Isle, Louisiana, on a barrier island covered in sea grass, white oleander, and wild hibiscus, where white pelicans nest and roseate spoonbills hang out, near the sand dunes on a spit of land known as Elmer's Island, my family has a fish camp. It's a double-wide trailer built up on stilts overlooking the marsh.

Fishing is part and parcel of Cajun life. Right after my mom had my baby brother, Nathaniel, when he was just weeks old, Maw Maw Toups insisted everybody come to the camp. "With a newborn? No, we can't go," Mama said. But Maw Maw Toups wouldn't have it. *You've got a baby? Tough.* So she came and picked everyone up herself. We were going fishing, dammit.

Maw Maw Toups lived with a rod and reel in her hand. The last ten years of her life, she fished nearly every day. She was even fishing on Grand Isle with my dad the day before Katrina hit. The hurricane was supposed to be heading far east, to Mississippi and Alabama, and they were at the bait shack looking for shrimp when some of the old salts said the water didn't look good. So even though the weathermen were all predicting a wide berth to the east, the old guys scurried to move their boats north. They sold their bait shrimp—Daddy bought nearly 300 pounds for $2 a pound—and some were even trying to sell their boats.

But if the fish are biting, you fish. And that's what Maw Maw Toups and Daddy did. Right up until they had to get the hell out of Dodge— and got stuck in standstill evacuation traffic.

Hurricanes don't mess around. Back in the 1800s, Grand Isle had huge hotels and a train coming through it. It was a thriving resort town. They used to grow cotton and sugarcane. Before the Mississippi River changed course in the 1880s, the mouth came out near here, around Bayou La Fouche. This is where my ancestors settled, the coastal Cajuns, in the 1700s. Then the hurricane of 1896 wiped it all out.

Mama didn't grow up with a fishing family; she married into it. Vacations were always at the fish camp. Before we had a place down here, often somebody would offer use of their camp to our family. Daddy insists they were all "nice" places. But Mama put her foot down after we went to a shack in Toledo Bend where the grass was growing six feet tall and she discovered a massive king snake on one of the beds.

It was cold—winter hadn't worn off yet—so the snake was dormant. And king snakes are harmless. But it was huge. She said, "We're going home and we're never coming back."

So after that, we stayed in nicer places. But by "nicer," let's remember, our current camp is a double-wide on stilts.

These days, when we get to the camp, the first thing Daddy does is set out crab traps. Then we head out for a day of fishing and come home to a mess of crabs. He takes that first catch and makes a really good crab stew. This is strictly camp food; I've never seen him make it anywhere else. First he gives the crabs a quick poach so they're easy to handle. Then he breaks the shells, removes the lungs, breaks the bodies in half, and cooks a dark roux stew. The crabmeat dissolves out of the bodies while the stew cooks. Three hours later it's got so much flavor it makes you want to cry for Jesus. You serve it with a coffee cup (that's what we refer to as a "camp ladle") into bowls with rice, picking up the bodies to suck the juice out of the shells as you eat. After a long day of fishing it's the perfect thing.

Normally we go for redfish or trout down here. But we can find a way to cook near about anything. Sheepshead. Sailtop catfish. You name it. The important thing is to catch them.

I learned early on that when the fish are biting, you don't stop. One day down in Grand Isle the fish were just jumping in the boat. But I got seasick. Puking everywhere. Daddy steered the boat toward the beach of Elmer's Island and got to water shallow enough for wading—and then he threw me out of the damn boat. He told me to wade through the surf, walk over the sand dune, cross the road, and that camp would be just on the other side.

Mama was *real* mad at him about throwing me overboard. But I get it. We were catching fish. Cajun life doesn't stop just for you.

BLUE CRAB CAMP STEW

At our camp, my dad always puts out crab traps. And if we're lucky, we wind up with a shit-ton of blue crab before the weekend is over. The crab boil might get top billing at the fish camp, but this crab stew from my dad is the stuff that'll make you all tingly. It's a little different every time because it all depends on what the hell we've got on hand. We don't always hit the grocery shopping just right. Especially if Mama isn't there. So, if we've only got frozen prepackaged trinity? Sure. Or no bell peppers? Hell, just use some sweet peppers. Not enough onion? Stretch it. Basically, just make sure you've got around 2 cups of trinity. And if we've got crawfish—who am I kidding? We always have crawfish—we'll throw the tails in. As long as you've got crab, roux, and fish stock, you can't go wrong. The rest is just beautiful lagniappe. | *Serves 6 to 8*

½ cup vegetable oil

½ cup all-purpose flour

1 medium onion, diced

1 red bell pepper, diced

2 ribs celery, diced

4 cloves garlic, minced

7 cups Easy Seafood Stock (page 15), or store-bought fish stock

12 to 18 medium-size blue crabs (about 4 pounds), scalded, cleaned, and broken into halves (see next page)

½ pound crawfish tail meat (optional)

2 teaspoons hot sauce

2 teaspoons kosher salt

½ teaspoon ground black pepper

Everyday Rice (page 17), for serving

› In a large heavy-bottomed pan (like a 13-quart Dutch oven) over medium heat, make a Caramel-Colored Roux (page 10) using the oil and flour, about 30 minutes. My dad calls this a dark roux, but my normal dark roux is darker, more like chocolate. This one is a little less intense for the seafood. Once the roux is a caramel color, add the trinity (onion, pepper, celery). Sweat the vegetables in the roux, stirring regularly, for about 5 minutes, until the onions are translucent. Add the garlic, stir, and cook 1 minute.

› Add the stock. Turn up the heat to bring to a rolling boil, then reduce the heat to low and simmer uncovered for about an hour.

› Add the cleaned crabs with any crab fat (aka crab roe) and the crawfish, if using, and cook on medium-low for 30 minutes.

› Add the hot sauce, salt, and pepper—just season to taste. Serve with rice.

CLEANING CRABS

We always start with live crabs. So before you can begin the stew you've got to scald the crabs and clean them. Fill a large pot (big enough to fit 24 crabs) with water and bring to a boil. Drop the live crabs in the pot and cook for 1 minute to scald them. You just need to cook them long enough so you can clean them. Here's my dad's easy method:

Using your hands, remove the claws and legs from the body, and then remove the carapace from the body. With the back of a butter knife, scrape the lungs from the body and discard. Use the knife to scrape and discard the mandibles (or as I like to say, the crab's face). With kitchen shears, remove the leg knuckles. Now you're good to go. Throw them in the pot.

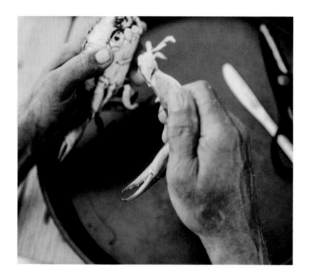
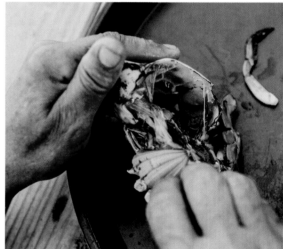
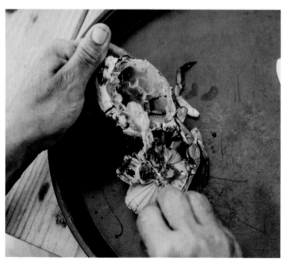

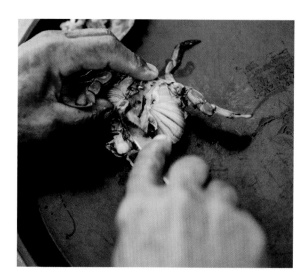

CAJUN QUESO
(CRAB FONDUE)

I know people who say you shouldn't mix cheese and seafood. I say, screw those rules. I refuse to live in a fascist culinary world. Those people have clearly never had Parmesan atop broiled oysters. That shit is good. They've also clearly never had my fondue.

This is not a fondue in the traditional sense. Normally you'd warm up your cheese and wine and whiskey and dust in a little flour. Instead, this is a béchamel sauce with all the components of fondue, just combined in a different order. I use my Pepper Paste of Pain instead of traditional kirschwasser because I like a little more acid and some heat. | *Serves 6 to 8*

4 tablespoons (½ stick) unsalted butter	1 teaspoon Isaac's Pepper Paste of Pain (page 21) or hot sauce	1 cup grated Gruyère cheese
3 tablespoons all-purpose flour	1 teaspoon kosher salt	1 pound lump crabmeat (or crawfish tails or chopped poached shrimp)
¼ cup dry white wine	¼ teaspoon white pepper	Baguette, crudités, or tortilla chips, for serving
2 cups whole milk	¼ teaspoon saffron	

Note: I use Gruyère for the cheese here, but even mozzarella would work, or cheddar. A cup of Velveeta would be fine. Or a packet of pre-shredded Colby. That's what we might have at fish camp. If you want to go high-end, use a super-funky Époisses and serve alongside some beef skewers.

› Melt the butter on low in a large saucepan. Cook, without allowing the butter to brown, until the milk solids are cooked out. Once the butter stops foaming, whisk in the flour. Cook on low heat about a minute, stirring once. You're taking a white roux to blonde (see page 9), and it'll happen pretty quick.

› Add the wine and stir continuously for about 30 seconds. Still stirring constantly with the whisk, add the milk in a thin stream. If you walk away for even a second, you will get lumpy béchamel and no one will be impressed with your cooking. Once it all comes together, thickens slightly, and emulsifies (about 3 to 5 minutes), it's okay to stop stirring continuously, but give it a good turn every minute from here on out, about 10 minutes more, until the mixture is smooth.

› Add the pepper paste, salt, white pepper, and saffron and stir well. Bring it up to a bare simmer, stirring with the whisk occasionally. Consistency should be that of, well, fondue. If it gets too thick, you can add another little splash of milk. Once the roux has cooked and there's no floury taste, about 10 minutes, remove from heat and stir in the cheese. Add the crabmeat (or other seafood of your choice). Adjust salt to taste.

› Serve with sides of crusty baguette or crudités. Or with tortilla or corn chips like queso.

STUFFED CRAB

Everywhere in south Louisiana where you can get a fried seafood platter—those creaky places with grease stains on the ceiling—they have stuffed crab (served in thin little metal tins) that's mostly breadcrumbs and tons of other filler. But come on, man, let the crab speak for itself. You don't need that sawdust breadcrumb bullshit. My version is just crab and herbs, with a little mayonnaise to bind it. I want the crab to sing. And though this recipe is for stuffed whole crabs, if you can't get them whole, you can still make some damn fine crab cakes. | *Serves 6*

1 pound jumbo lump crabmeat (from about 6 crabs), picked through for shells

3 tablespoons mayonnaise

1 bunch green onions, green parts only, thinly sliced

2 tablespoons finely chopped fresh parsley

Grated zest and about 2 tablespoons juice of 2 lemons

1½ teaspoons kosher salt

¼ teaspoon cayenne pepper

2 teaspoons unsalted butter, melted, but not hot

½ cup unseasoned breadcrumbs, divided

6 whole crab shells or 6 small ramekins, for serving

› Preheat the oven to 350°F. In a large mixing bowl, combine the crabmeat, mayonnaise, green onions, parsley, lemon juice and zest, salt, and cayenne. With a rubber spatula, gently fold the mixture together. Since you're using jumbo lump crab, the last thing you want to do is rough it all up and tear the meat. Once the ingredients are combined, drizzle in the melted butter and then immediately give it another fold to incorporate. Because the rest of the ingredients are cold, that butter will seize up quickly, so you want to fold it in as soon as you pour it, still being as gentle as you can. At this point, you have a really good crab salad that can be served cold on its own, or used for crab cakes (page 169).

› Add ¼ cup of the breadcrumbs and fold gently to mix. Divide the crab and breadcrumb mixture evenly among the 6 crab shells. Sprinkle the remaining ¼ cup breadcrumbs equally on top of each crab shell.

› Place the crab shells on a baking sheet and bake until the internal temperature is 130°F, about 30 minutes. Using a good thermometer is crucial here because you really just want to warm it all up. If the mixture gets too hot, the mayonnaise will break and you'll just end up with greasy crab.

CRAB CAKES

These are great for a light lunch with a salad and a little aioli. Did I say fried crab cakes for a light lunch? Why yes I did. It makes sense to me. | *Serves 6*

Crab mixture (through the first step) from Stuffed Crab (page 166)

2 cups all-purpose flour

2 teaspoons kosher salt, divided

2 cups buttermilk

2 large eggs

2 cups unseasoned breadcrumbs

3 cups peanut oil

Cane Vinegar Aioli (page 19), for serving

› Line a baking sheet with parchment paper. Divide the crab mixture into six 3-ounce portions (you can pack the mixture into a 3-ounce ladle for easy weighing and shaping). Shape each into a sort of hockey-puck shape and divvy out on the lined baking sheet. Gently cover the baking sheet with plastic wrap and place in the freezer for 1 hour.

› Meanwhile, prepare three mixing bowls: one with the flour and 1 teaspoon salt, one with the buttermilk and eggs whisked together, and one with the breadcrumbs and 1 teaspoon salt.

› Remove the crab cakes from freezer. The outsides should be fairly hard, but the cakes should feel soft inside when pressed. Working quickly so as not to warm the crab, gently dip each crab cake in the flour mixture, then the buttermilk-egg mixture, then the breadcrumbs.

› Set on a wire rack until they are all breaded. Place the rack back in the refrigerator for 20 minutes.

› When ready to fry, fill a 10-inch cast iron skillet halfway with the peanut oil. It may take a little less than 3 cups. When pan-frying, you want the oil to come halfway up the crab cake. Heat the oil over medium heat until it is 350°F.

› After 20 minutes, remove the rack from the fridge. Working in two batches, place 3 crab cakes in the 350°F oil and pan-fry for 3 minutes on each side, until golden brown. Handle them gently when placing them in the oil, flipping them, and removing them so they don't fall apart. Once they begin to break apart they totally explode in the pan. It's pretty embarrassing, and that's a waste of some damn good crab. Fry until they reach an internal temperature of 130°F.

› Remove from the oil and drain on a wire rack for 1 minute. Serve with the aioli.

DR. BRENT TOUPS'
SEAFOOD GUMBO

You might want to master your roux and perfect a good ole Gumbo #1 (page 106) before you tackle this one. Not because it's hard, but because if you don't live near water and harvest your own seafood like an old Cajun coot, this can easily be a $350 pot of gumbo. You don't want to make a crappy roux and ruin a car payment's worth of seafood. I'd kick your ass for that.

When Daddy is really going crazy, he fills a giant stockpot up to the brim with every type of seafood he can get his hands on. Especially if we've had a good day down at the camp pulling in wild oysters from the beds, crabs from the traps, and a net full of shrimp. But if we're buying the seafood and you're invited over to eat, count your blessings. Someone in the house really likes you. | *Serves 8 to 10*

- 1 cup neutral vegetable oil, like canola or grapeseed
- 1 cup all-purpose flour
- 1 medium onion, finely diced
- 1 medium bell pepper, finely diced
- 4 ribs celery, finely diced
- 2 bay leaves

- 4 cloves garlic, minced
- ¾ cup V8 or other tomato juice
- 2 quarts Easy Seafood Stock (page 15) or fish stock
- 2 tablespoons Crack Spice (page 18) or Cajun/Creole seasoning
- 1 quart shucked oysters, with liquid

- 1 pound lump crabmeat, picked through for shells
- 1 pound claw crabmeat
- 2 pounds medium shrimp (about 80 shrimp), peeled and deveined
- Everyday Rice (page 17), for serving

› In a Dutch oven or large stockpot over medium heat, make a dark roux (page 10), using the oil and flour, about 45 minutes. Once the roux is the color of dark caramel, add the onion, bell pepper, celery, and bay leaves and stir vigorously for about 5 minutes, to soften the vegetables and caramelize. Add the garlic and cook for an additional minute, stirring often. Add the V8 juice and stir often for about 5 minutes. (The V8 is Daddy's way to turn it into a brick roux, page 10. I'd typically use tomato paste, but I don't mess with his method in his recipes.)

› Add the stock and bring to a simmer. Simmer for 10 minutes to make sure the flour in the roux is well cooked. Add the crack spice. Bring to a boil, then reduce to a simmer and cook uncovered for 20 minutes.

› Add all of the seafood and quickly bring back to a boil over high heat. Once it's boiling, reduce to a simmer and cook uncovered for 25 more minutes, until oysters and shrimp are cooked through.

› Serve in bowls over rice.

CITRUS AND SEAFOOD

Maw Maw Toups, the fishing queen of our family, always said that you should eat a citrus dessert after a seafood meal to cleanse the palate. You don't want chocolate after your crabmeat. You want something clean and refreshing. I abide by her rule to this day, with whatever citrus I've got on hand. That might be a mixed citrus parfait or a lemon icebox pie. And when satsumas, the sweet mandarin oranges that grow like crazy in south Louisiana, are coming in, we might just peel and eat 'em at the table.

CRAB FAT RICE

Crab fat is the roe of female crabs. It's extremely fatty and, for some reason, around here *crab fat* sounds better than *crab roe*. It's all about perception. Foie gras? Sure! But fatty liver from a force-fed duck? Get the hell away from me.

I was first introduced to crab fat when a chef buddy from the Lowcountry made me she-crab soup. So I played around with crab fat for years (I once made crab fat gnocchi I couldn't give away) but couldn't make anything work. Then I needed a dish to go with couvillion (page 184) and I tried crab fat rice. It worked beautifully. The end result should be creamy, almost like risotto, not broken up like fried rice. If it starts to look like fried rice, you've kept it over the heat too long and should add a little water to bring back the creaminess. | *Serves 6 to 8*

½ cup water

1 cup Crab Fat Butter (recipe follows)

4 cups cooked white rice

2 bunches green onions, green tops only, finely sliced

Kosher salt

› Combine the water and crab fat butter in a large cold skillet. Heat the skillet over low heat, stirring occasionally, until the butter has melted and dissolved into the water, but is not boiling. (It's important to keep the heat low so the butter doesn't break.) Gently fold in the rice over low heat, stirring occasionally until warmed, about 3 minutes. Mix in the green onions. Adjust salt to taste and serve.

CRAB FAT BUTTER

How do you get crab fat? Well, first you can buy it. Look for crab roe at seafood markets and some specialty Asian markets. But to harvest it yourself: Crack open the carapace of the female crab. Right below the lungs are these little golden nuggets. That's what you want. Scoop 'em out. Most people have already been eating crab fat without knowing what it is, or throwing it away because they think it's guts (poor bastards). My mama likes the roe better than she likes crabmeat. When I bust open a big crab, I always share a hunk of the crab roe with Mama. This recipe makes more than you'll need for Crab Fat Rice, but it freezes well. I keep some on hand to use for future batches of Crab Fat Rice, roasting oysters (page 184), adding to scrambled eggs, buttering biscuits, or even with a plate of pasta. | *Makes 2 pounds*

1 pound crab fat (from about 20 to 30 female crabs)

1 pound unsalted butter, cut into 1-inch cubes, softened

2 tablespoons minced garlic

1 cup white wine

Grated zest of 2 lemons

2 teaspoons ground Aleppo pepper (or paprika or crushed red pepper flakes)

2 teaspoons ground white pepper

1 teaspoon kosher salt

› Manually push the crab fat through a drum sieve or fine mesh colander to remove all shell particles. Chill the crab fat in the fridge until ready to work with it.

› In a small skillet, melt one of the 1-inch cubes of butter over medium heat. Add the garlic and sweat for 2 minutes, until aromatic. Add the wine and cook over medium heat until it reduces to 2 tablespoons. Remove from the heat and cool to room temperature.

› Transfer the reduced wine mixture to a stand mixer bowl. Add the crab fat, remaining butter cubes, lemon zest, Aleppo pepper, white pepper, and salt. Fit the stand mixer with the paddle attachment (don't use a hand beater with a whisk!), and mix on medium speed for 30 seconds, until all ingredients are well incorporated, scraping down the sides once or twice. You just want to mix the butter, not whip it. (If you don't have a stand mixer, you can mix it together by hand with a rubber spatula.) It's done as soon as you don't see any chunks of plain butter.

› You can use it immediately or save it by packing into a Tupperware container, rolling into logs in

plastic wrap like cookie dough, or placing in a ramekin covered tightly with plastic wrap. In the fridge, it'll last for a week but it freezes well when formed into logs and wrapped tightly with plastic. You can pull it out, slice off what you need, and put it back in the freezer for up to 3 months.

RAW OYSTERS

Oysters taste like the area where they're grown and vary in flavor from coast to coast and bayou to bayou. Some come out of the water salty as hell. Others could stand a little bump-bump time with a salt lick. So when I get oysters, I shuck and eat one straight off to see what I'm dealing with. If it needs salt, I add some to the mignonette. A good mignonette complements the flavor of an oyster without hiding it.

To shuck an oyster, you need an oyster knife, a cut-proof glove, and a kitchen towel.

Put the glove on your non-dominant hand and hold the knife in the other. Place an oyster, cup side down, in a towel that's been folded twice and hold in your non-dom hand. Insert the knife tip into the hinge of the oyster. Focus pressure on the hinge, and using an up-and-down motion with the knife, pop the oyster open, being careful not to puncture the meat. Wipe the blade off and, from the back, shimmy the knife to open the shell a little while sliding it to the front. Peek in the oyster and locate the adductor "eye" and scrape the shell to cut it loose from the top shell. Repeat the same maneuver on the bottom shell. You get good after about 1,000 of these—so start shucking, you bad mutha shucka.

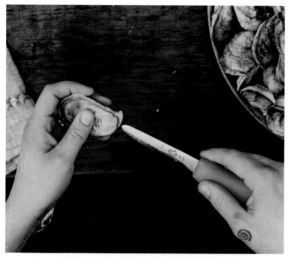

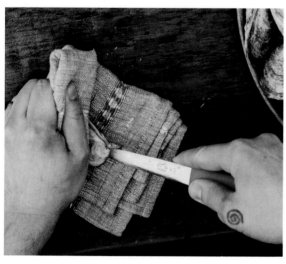

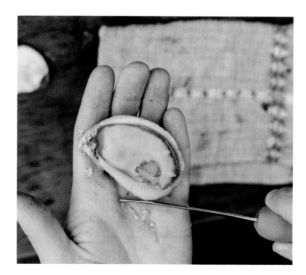

BOURÉ

Bouré is like poker crossed with spades. In this game, the betting is all done ahead of time, but that doesn't mean it's cheap to play. Let's say the buy-in is a dollar. Everybody antes up a dollar to play. Everybody gets five cards. Just like in poker you can trade in your cards. With bouré the dealer changes every hand, and he flips over his last card dealt—that suit is the trump card. So the dealer always has a trump card. The person to left of dealer starts. He plays a card. Let's say the trump suit is hearts. If the first player throws out the ace of spades, everybody has to play a spade. If you don't have a spade, you trump. If you lie and play a trump card even if you have a spade, and you get caught, then you forfeit that hand and have to match whatever is in the pot. Whoever wins the most hands wins the pot. You get five chances in a game (five cards) to win a hand. If it's a tie for the number of hands won, nobody wins the pot. The money stays in. If you bouré—meaning you don't win any hands—you match the pot. So if the pot's $4, you gotta put $4 straight in. You don't want to bouré at all. Throughout the game, you can easily see the pot double up, triple up, quadruple up—and then you bouré. So while it's not as exciting as poker when it comes to incremental betting, there's still the potential to get royally fucked. It's a fun game.

LEMON DASHI MIGNONETTE

I didn't grow up putting mignonette on oysters. We just weren't that fancy. But I sing the song of acid, and I love how a good mignonette balances the flavor of an oyster. I've been to restaurants where there's a bottle of vinegar on the table, and growing up we always had little bowls of flavored vinegar for crawfish boils (see Super Sauce, page 83)—I just never thought of any of that as "mignonette." Now that I'm all grown up and do chef shit, not only do I make mignonette, but I out-fancy myself by adding a little dashi to the mix. | *Makes about 1 cup*

- 1 cup fresh-squeezed lemon juice, strained to remove seeds and pulp
- 2 teaspoons sugar
- 1 teaspoon Hondashi (see Note, page 83)
- ½ teaspoon ground black pepper
- Kosher salt to taste

› Whisk all the ingredients together until the salt and sugar have dissolved. Adjust the salt level to your particular oysters and spoon ¼ teaspoon on each. A little drizzle is plenty.

SHERRY VINEGAR MIGNONETTE

With just a few ingredients, this is the easiest mignonette to make. There's a reason it's a classic. It's worth splurging on a nice aged sherry vinegar because the ingredients shine through here. | *Makes about 1 cup*

- 1 cup aged sherry vinegar
- ¼ cup finely minced shallot (1 big Louisiana shallot, or 2 smaller pink shallots)
- ½ teaspoon ground black pepper
- Kosher salt to taste

› Whisk all the ingredients together until the salt has dissolved. Adjust the salt level to your particular oysters and spoon ¼ teaspoon on each.

CHILE-MARINATED CRAB CLAWS

Crab claws are synonymous with south Louisiana. All along the coast, everybody loves their crab claws. I use some ingredients here that you don't usually see together—but they totally work. A good amount of acid, some salt, and some herbs make quality crab claws go all the way around. | *Serves 4*

14 tablespoons (⅞ cup) lemon juice (from about 10 lemons)

6 tablespoons lime juice (from about 9 limes)

¼ cup sherry vinegar

1 tablespoon hot sauce

2 tablespoons finely minced fresh ginger

1 jalapeño, seeded and minced (or your favorite hot pepper)

2 teaspoons sugar

2 teaspoons kosher salt

1 pound raw blue crab claws

8 cherry tomatoes, halved, for serving

½ cup Pickled Grilled Pineapple (page 142), for serving

› In a large nonreactive mixing bowl, combine the lemon juice, lime juice, vinegar, hot sauce, ginger, jalapeño, sugar, and salt and stir until the sugar and salt dissolve. Add the crab claws, making sure they are submerged.

› Chill for 30 minutes in the refrigerator. Remove from the fridge, toss in the cherry tomatoes and pickled pineapple, and serve.

THE BULLSHIT THRESHOLD

Well before there were "zero fucks" to give, Brent Toups would let us know that his give-a-shit factor was low. And we knew to believe him. No sense whining about anything around Daddy. And definitely not if there were fish to be caught.

DRUNKEN SHRIMP

This is a great, quick way to serve beautiful fresh head-on shrimp. Got someone coming over in 20 minutes? This is your go-to. Just try and dupe someone else into peeling the shrimp.

Don't be afraid of the heads—they really make this dish. You don't have to serve them with the heads on if you're a big old scaredy-cat. But when you're cooking them, gently crush the heads with the back of a spoon. This squeezes out a lot of extra flavor that amps up the dish. | *Serves 2 to 3*

1 teaspoon fennel seed

1 teaspoon black peppercorns

1 teaspoon ground Aleppo pepper (or paprika or crushed red pepper flakes)

½ tablespoon kosher salt

1½ pounds extra jumbo shrimp (about 16 to 20 shrimp per pound), peeled and deveined

2 tablespoons neutral vegetable oil, like canola or grapeseed

2 garlic cloves, minced

2 tablespoons chopped fresh oregano

¼ cup dry white wine

1 cup shrimp stock (or unsalted fish stock or Easy Seafood Stock, page 15)

10 cherry tomatoes, halved

4 tablespoons (½ stick) unsalted butter, softened and cut into ½-inch pieces

Juice of 1 lemon (about 2 tablespoons)

Everyday Rice (page 17), for serving

Note: If you want to make this for a group, instead of an intimate dinner, just double the recipe. You won't be able to fit 3 pounds of shrimp in a single pan, so use two pans or cook them in batches.

› In a small nonstick pan, toast the fennel seed and black pepper over medium-low heat until aromatic, about 3 minutes. Allow to cool and then grind in a spice grinder. In a bowl, combine the ground fennel and black pepper with the Aleppo pepper and salt. Lay the shrimp on a baking sheet and generously season both sides with the pepper mixture.

› Heat the oil in a large heavy skillet or Dutch oven over medium-high heat. Add the shrimp and sear for 1½ minutes. Flip the shrimp, add the garlic and oregano, and cook for 10 seconds. Deglaze the pan with the white wine, being sure to stir with a spoon to the bottom of the pan.

› Add the stock and tomatoes and cook until they are heated through. Crush the shrimp heads with the back of a spoon to release the juices. Remove from the heat and fold in the butter and lemon juice, quickly but gently. Serve over rice.

FRENCH BREAD–FRIED OYSTERS

This was the first oyster dish I ever made that I was really proud of. I came up with it during my very first days as a baby sous chef, back at age 24 in New Orleans. It's basically a deconstructed po'boy that still has some self-respect. Now, I love po'boys so much my cat is named Oyster Po'Boy Toups. And I don't like when people fuck around with a good po'boy. Just load me up a ton of oysters in our local Leidenheimer bread, and serve it with mayo, lettuce, hot sauce, and some pickles. My beard is always full of crumbs by the end of the adventure.

But the rest of that loaf of French bread honestly sucks the next day. So I wanted to do an oyster po'boy that wasn't a sandwich: French Bread–Fried Oysters. I like a lot of nekkid things, but a po'boy isn't one of them—so I give it a mayo aioli and add a tomato and onion salad.

When you fry the oysters, do not bread them ahead of time. Once you bread them, fry them up within the next few minutes. If you let them sit around, no matter how boss of a fryer you are, you'll never get the same texture. | *Serves 4*

2 quarts peanut oil

2 cups all-purpose flour

1 tablespoon popcorn salt, divided

2 large eggs

1 cup buttermilk

3 cups French Bread Breadcrumbs (see sidebar) or unseasoned breadcrumbs

20 oysters, chilled and shucked (see page 174)

Cane Vinegar Aioli (page 19), for serving

Red Onion and Tomato Salad (recipe follows), for serving

Note: Before you add salt, taste one of your oysters. If it's really salty, you can omit salt from the flour mixture. Down here, the wild oysters aren't very salty at all, so I add some to the flour.

› Heat the peanut oil in fryer or a large Dutch oven set over medium-high heat to 350°F. It's key for the oil to be fully preheated before you fry, or the oysters will get greasy. (While the oil is heating, you can make the Red Onion and Tomato Salad.)

› Set out three separate mixing bowls. In one, combine the flour and ½ tablespoon popcorn salt (if needed). In the second, whisk together the eggs and buttermilk until well combined. In the third, combine the breadcrumbs and remaining ½ tablespoon popcorn salt.

› In small batches, about 10 at a time, dip each oyster in the flour, then the egg wash, then the breadcrumbs. The trick is to use one hand for your dry stuff and one hand for your wet stuff—this will keep your hand from caking up. Once they have been dipped in breadcrumbs, set on resting rack until all 10 have been breaded.

› Deep-fry the oysters for 1 to 2 minutes, depending on the size, until firm and golden brown. Remove from the oil and drain on paper towels while you prepare and cook the remaining 10 oysters.

› These are fancy oysters, so here's how you assemble your plate: For each oyster, put a tablespoon of the aioli on a plate. Place a single fried oyster on top of each dollop. Put a small pinch of tomato salad on top. (Or just make a pile of fried oysters and tomato salad atop a smear of aioli.) Enjoy your fancy fried oysters, you fancy beast.

RED ONION AND TOMATO SALAD

Serves 4

2 Roma (plum) tomatoes,
   halved lengthwise, seeds and
   gelatinous center removed

1 medium red onion, peeled

1 teaspoon sherry vinegar

1 teaspoon horseradish
   (preferably freshly grated)

½ teaspoon kosher salt

¼ teaspoon ground black
   pepper

› Julienne the tomato halves and the onion, cutting each into slivers of about the same size. Combine the tomatoes, onion, sherry vinegar, horseradish, salt, and pepper in a mixing bowl. Toss until well mixed.

FRENCH BREAD BREADCRUMBS

Leidenheimer is the quintessential New Orleans bread—the best po'boy bread you'll ever find. But after one day, it's worthless. Stale, dry, not worth a damn. However, stale French bread makes the best breadcrumbs—and Leidenheimer ships. Cut the loaf into 1-inch slices, place on a baking sheet in your oven, and dry on the lowest setting for about an hour. You want to dry it until the bread snaps easily, but doesn't have any color. You're not making toast. If you have a gas oven, you can put the slices in there with just the pilot light lit overnight, and they will be perfect. Pulse the dried bread in a food processor for about 10 seconds until it's mostly the consistency of grains of sand. The breadcrumbs will keep in an airtight container for several weeks. Use them for French Bread–Fried Oysters, Stuffed Crab (page 166), or anywhere else you need breadcrumbs.

ROASTED OYSTERS WITH CRAB FAT BUTTER

I came up with this idea while I was standing on the banks at the fish camp cracking open raw oysters with my knife. I looked around and thought, "I want to build a fire!" I got the fire cranking on the ground and then set up a few bricks around it. I balanced a grate on the top and let my inner beast roar. Man! Fire! Oysters!

I've adapted this recipe to the oven for those less likely to succumb to bestial tendencies. But you can also do them on a super-hot grill. Just be sure to arrange the oysters on the grate so they don't tip over—the Crab Fat Butter will light the grill on fire. And then you'll have a fun story about how you ruined the oysters. | *Serves 4*

---

6 tablespoons Crab Fat Butter (page 173)

1 dozen oysters, shucked (see page 174), still in shell with oyster liquor

6 teaspoons unseasoned breadcrumbs

Rock or kosher salt

Pickled Jalapeños (page 139), for serving (optional)

› Turn the broiler to high and allow to preheat. You want your oven piping hot before you put them in.

› Put ½ tablespoon Crab Fat Butter on top of each oyster. It works better if you cut off thin slices of butter and not put it on in a big clump. Top each with ½ teaspoon breadcrumbs.

› Line a rimmed baking sheet with rock salt to stabilize the oysters and keep them from tipping over. Hell, you can use dried beans. Anything to keep them stable.

Nestle the oysters in the salt on the baking sheet, making sure they don't touch or overlap.

› Put them under the broiler for 6 to 8 minutes, but keep an eye on them pretty much the whole time. As soon as the oysters have tightened and the edges start to curl, they are ready.

› Serve immediately. I like mine with a slice of pickled jalapeño.

QUICK-POACHED SHRIMP

This is the perfect way to cook shrimp to put out for a party that's not a backyard shrimp boil. This is also how my kids prefer to eat shrimp—finger food time! Served with a little aioli (page 19), a little Cocktail Sauce (page 83)—they're perfect. You can multiply this recipe to make more for a bigger group. | *Serves 4*

12 cups water

2 cups rice wine vinegar

1 cup sugar

⅔ cup kosher salt

8 cloves garlic, minced

5 bay leaves

1 pound extra jumbo shrimp (about 16 to 20), peeled and deveined

4 cups ice

› Combine the water, vinegar, sugar, salt, garlic, and bay leaves in a stockpot and bring to a rolling boil over high heat. Add the shrimp and cook for 2 minutes. Drain the shrimp, reserving 1 cup of the cooking liquid. Place the shrimp in a nonreactive bowl with the cooking liquid and the ice. Using your hand or a spoon, toss the shrimp, liquid, and ice together and allow to sit for 3 minutes. It's not a big deal if they aren't ice cold; you just want to stop the cooking process—and if they sit in the water too long, they get mushy. There are few things worse in this life than mushy shrimp. Drain the shrimp thoroughly and pat dry.

› Eat right away or put in the fridge to chill until serving. They're best if you eat them within 24 hours.

PICKLED SHRIMP

There's not a whole lot of ingredients in this recipe list because when you have great shrimp, like we do in south Louisiana, you want to let those babies shine. The rice wine vinegar gives the perfect punch because it has a little sugar in it—it's very calm and not astringent. These shrimp are well seasoned and you get a hit of acidity, but they still taste like shrimp. | *Serves 4*

- 1 cup rice wine vinegar
- ¼ cup sugar
- 1 tablespoon kosher salt
- 1 cup lemon juice
- 1 cup lime juice
- 1 pound chilled Quick-Poached Shrimp (page 188)

› In a small saucepan, combine the vinegar, sugar, and salt and warm over medium heat until the salt and sugar are fully dissolved. Remove from the heat and refrigerate until thoroughly chilled. (You can leave it in the saucepot or transfer it to any nonreactive vessel while refrigerating.)

› Once the vinegar mixture is cold, stir in the lemon and lime juice and mix well. Pour into a 9 x 13-inch baking dish (or anything large enough to hold the shrimp in a single layer). Submerge the shrimp in the liquid, spreading them out in a single layer. Cover with plastic wrap and let marinate in the refrigerator for 12 hours.

› Drain, reserving ½ cup of the marinade. Transfer pickled shrimp and reserved marinade to a bowl, jar, or shallow rimmed platter and serve.

LIQUID AIR CONDITIONER

This is my favorite 9 o'clock shot. 9 p.m. Not 9 a.m.—that's a different shot. When I've been sweating all damn day in the kitchen, I want something to cool me down that's not too strong (because I've got to keep working). It also works if I'm hot from a day out in the blazing sun trying to catch fish. I mix together equal parts crème de menthe and vodka and shake the hell out of it over ice. Pour it up and drink it down. You'll go from "aughhhh" to "ahhhh" in 30 seconds. It's refreshing, not too sweet, icy, and has a minty cooling effect. It feels like an air conditioner blasting your body from the inside out.

BOAT CEVICHE

We had so much ceviche when I was little that I thought it was a traditional Cajun dish. My dad loved it, and he would always make it when we were out on the boat. He would even make a little ceviche kit and bring it with us in a Tupperware. If we caught a fish, he'd clean and cut it up, then toss with the ingredients from his kit in the Tupperware. Twenty minutes later, we'd pile it on tortilla chips and shovel it in our mouths right there on the water.

Any young, sweet, white-fleshed fish—like red snapper, drum, redfish, speckled trout—works great for this, so use whatever's available. Larger fish like mahi mahi or amberjack work in a pinch. It's also really good with shrimp. Luckily we've never had to use the bait shrimp. That would have meant it was a really bad fishing day. | *Serves 6*

Grated zest of 4 lemons, plus ¾ cup juice

Grated zest of 5 limes plus ¾ cup juice (from about 6 limes)

2 tablespoons white wine vinegar

1 red onion, finely diced

½ bunch cilantro (including stems), chiffonaded (about ½ cup)

1 jalapeño, seeded and finely minced

1½ tablespoons kosher salt

1 pound fish filets (or a mixture of fish filets and shrimp)

Note: This also makes a great lunch salad. Toss some greens with a pile of ceviche, and add a glug of olive oil. Killer.

› Combine everything except the fish and mix well. If you're making this on a boat, make it all in a Tupperware. If you're making it at home, use a nonreactive bowl. Regardless of where you are, let the mixture sit in the fridge or cooler for at least 20 minutes before adding the fish: It needs time for the salt to extract the flavors of the cilantro and for all the flavors to meld.

› Meanwhile, dice the fish into ½-inch cubes. After 20 minutes, add the fish to the citrus mixture and toss well. Return to refrigerator or ice chest and chill for 10 minutes. Toss the fish to make sure everything is well coated, and chill for another 10 minutes—or until ready to serve, up to 24 hours.

› Be sure to eat the ceviche within 24 hours. I personally think it's the most magical at the 12-hour mark, but it never makes it that long. It's lucky if it makes it off the boat. To the hungry go the spoils.

› Serve with corn chips (I like Tostitos Scoops). Don't be a snob about it.

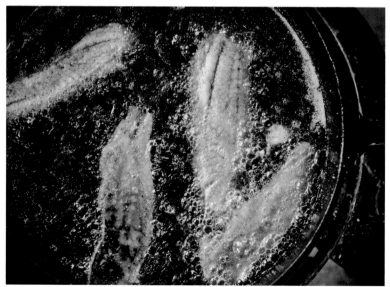

THE FISH FRY

If you catch enough fish (it's not always a given), a fish fry is inevitable. The usual suspects at the fish camp are snapper, drum, redfish, and my favorite, speckled trout. Forget plates and a table. We shovel it in with one hand, a cold beer in the other, while standing over the pile that's draining on paper towels. We dip the fish in ranch or Caesar or whatever dressing we've got a bottle of—or tartar sauce if we're feeling fancy. Never ketchup, though. Ketchup is for French fries. Or babies (because babies like ketchup; we don't eat babies, don't worry).

Once you've got fried fish, you've also got fish tacos. Take a tortilla (the bigass flour ones), lettuce, and Caesar or ranch dressing, and have yourself a Cajun taco. Hell yeah. | *Serves 4*

About 2 quarts peanut oil

3 cups corn flour (it's finer than corn meal and adheres better)

3 tablespoons popcorn salt

2 tablespoons onion powder

1 tablespoon ground white pepper

1 tablespoon granulated garlic

2 teaspoons cayenne pepper

1 teaspoon celery salt

2 pounds fish filets (about ½ inch thick or thinner), skin removed

EQUIPMENT
Deep fryer (or a large, deep cast iron skillet or Dutch oven)

› If using a deep fryer, fill with oil to the fill line. If using a cast iron skillet or Dutch oven, fill with peanut oil to a depth of 1½ inches. Heat the oil to 350°F over medium-high heat.

› In a ziplock bag or large Tupperware container with a lid (a ziplock is what we'd have at the camp; it's one less thing to wash), combine the corn flour, popcorn salt, onion powder, white pepper, granulated garlic, cayenne, and celery salt. Seal the bag or cover the container and give it a good shake to mix well.

› Add one-third of the filets to the bag or Tupperware. Seal and give the fish a good shake to coat well with the corn flour mixture. Remove the fish and shake the excess back into the bag. Gently lay the filets into the hot oil. I lay them in with my hand but the oil will pop a little bit. If you prefer to use tongs, you can; but be careful not to puncture the filets or remove any breading. Cook in the oil for 1 minute, until the fish is crispy and golden brown on both sides. If they're super thin, you likely don't need to turn them over, but if they are thicker, you might need to turn them (gently) with tongs to brown them evenly. Cook them until they have an internal temperature of 135°F, but I'll tell you, I have never once stuck a thermometer into a piece of fish. You just want it golden and crispy.

› Remove the fish with a spider or a large slotted metal spoon and place it on a wire rack or a plate with paper towels to drain. While the first batch is cooking, bread the second batch so it's ready to go as soon as the first batch comes out of the oil, and on with the third batch.

› Serve hot.

WHOLE SALT-BAKED FISH

Even though you're baking a whole fish in a mound of salt, it won't come out salty—the salt just seals in the juices. It's a very forgiving way of cooking fish. And though it might look complicated, it's not. I use redfish, but any white-fleshed mild fish will work. And if you've got a bigass pan, you can do this with a much larger fish, or a couple of them. You're really only limited by the size of the pan. | *Serves 2*

1 (2½-pound) whole fish, gutted, scaled, and fins removed—but leave the head and tail

1 lemon, cut into 6 round slices

4 large sprigs fresh thyme

4 bay leaves

2 cloves garlic, crushed

1 (3-pound) box kosher salt

4 large egg whites

2 tablespoons lemon juice

2 tablespoons extra virgin olive oil

½ teaspoon Dijon mustard

1 teaspoon kosher salt

½ teaspoon ground black pepper

› Preheat the oven to 400°F. Stuff the cavity of the fish with lemon slices, thyme, bay leaves, and garlic.

› In a large mixing bowl, mix the salt and egg whites with your hands; it will become the consistency of wet sand.

› In a large baking dish or rimmed baking sheet that is large enough to fit the entire fish (it's okay if the fish only just fits), lay one-third of the salt mixture down, roughly in the shape of the fish. Place the fish on top of the salt mixture and pack the remaining salt mixture around the fish, leaving exposed the area from the eyes to the nose, and also the tail fin. The salt mixture should fully encase the fish, but may not fill the pan. In fact, unless you use a really narrow pan, you'll probably leave most of the pan exposed.

› Bake for about 30 minutes, until the internal temperature of the fish is 130 to 135°F. Depending on the exact size of your fish, your cooking time may vary. Don't break the salt crust while it's cooking or you'll let the juices escape. If you have one of those nice thermometers with the wires that you can leave in the oven while you cook to determine temperature, use that, and pack the salt around the probe to seal it in before cooking. If you don't have one of those fancy thermometers, check the temp by going through the exposed mouth with a probe thermometer. Once done,

remove the fish from oven and let rest for 5 minutes before serving.

› While the fish is resting, whisk together the lemon juice, oil, Dijon, salt, and pepper to make a lemon vinaigrette to serve over the fish.

› To remove the fish from the salt shell, use a butter knife and a wooden mallet or spoon. Like a paleontologist, I try to guess where the dorsal fin would be. Hit the fish right there, in the middle of the back (remember it's laying on its side). I place the tip of the butter knife where the dorsal fin was and tap it with the mallet or spoon, putting it in and giving it a wiggle. I score all the way around the fish, like I'm excavating it, so I can remove the salt dome in one piece. It doesn't mess anything up if you don't get it off in the one piece, but it just looks cooler if you do. Once you've gone all the way around the outline of the fish, remove the top part of the salt dome.

› The skin is a little chewy, but it still tastes good, so help yourself to a piece. Cook's reward. Then go under the skin with a fork, down to the spine, and slide across the bottom to filet the fish from the spine. You might get it all in one filet. But most times you have to go back and clean it up.

› Then take the mallet and butter knife, and place the knife at the base of the spine where it meets the head.

Tap the handle end of the butter knife with the mallet to crack the spine. Remove the entire spine and bones. With a fork, slide along the bottom of the fish, between the flesh and the salt crust, to remove the other fish filet.

You probably won't get the skin off cleanly with this filet, and that's fine.

› This will yield two 10-ounce (or so) filets. Place each filet on a plate and spoon lemon vinaigrette on top.

THE HUNT CAMP

Boudreaux and Thibodeaux, they duck-huntin' and they comin' back
to the camp in their little motorized pirogue. A-run-da-din-din-din-
din-din-duhn. They run out of gas.

BOUDREAUX: Thibodeaux, you fill up the gas can?

THIBODEAUX: I thought you did.

They got no gas. But they can see the camp.

THIBODEAUX: We ain't got no paddles, we ain't got no gas, one of us is
gon' have to swim back.

BOUDREAUX: Man, fuck you. It's freezing fucking cold.

THIBODEAUX: I got an idea. I'm gon' shine this spotlight at the camp.
You walk across the light and go to the camp.

Boudreaux look at him, and says: "How dumb you think I am? I'm
gon' get halfways across and you gon' turn off the light."

Deer is my favorite wild game to eat, but not my favorite thing to hunt. Hunting deer is boring. Unless you're great at stalking—which you won't be if you haven't spent years living in the woods—you're sitting in a deer stand for four hours, freezing your dick off and trying to stay still. After a while you're like, "Yep, the scenery is beautiful, but goddamn."

I like hunting squirrel—you can practically do it in your backyard—but it's my least favorite to eat. A *sauce piquant* can make it nice, but it's still a squirrel. Duck is my favorite to hunt *and* eat. You get in a duck blind, smoke a joint, pass the whiskey, tell a few dirty jokes. Over a couple of hours, you might shoot two boxes of shells, and among the group, you always end up with some ducks…unless the ducks aren't flying, which sucks. But that's what I love about hunting. It's not a guaranteed thing. You're out there observing nature in its beautiful way—and then maybe shooting it out of the sky.

We go hunting primarily on swamp land or in rice fields, mostly south of I-10. Either you get invited to somebody's hunting lease or you pay somebody to go and hunt on their land. Sometimes Daddy would do someone's dental work for free, in exchange for a hunt.

My brother takes his daughters to the hunting camp and puts them in deer stands. You go, no matter how young you are. But if you're too young, you don't get a gun. And before you get a gun, you're trained in how to use it safely. I was under ten when I got my first gun, a crack barrel 20-gauge. A single shot gun. I killed my first deer at age 13. But I haven't killed one recently, that's for sure. I think someone's calling the deer to let them know I'm coming.

One time I was deer hunting with my little brother. We'd been going hard for three or four days and I hadn't shot anything. Nathaniel had already shot one, while playing on his iPad. Damn him. It was the last day, and already dark. Nathaniel comes to pick me up on the four-wheeler to take me back to camp. I'm riding in the back, and I see a rabbit. I pull my pistol out and tell Nate I'm gonna shoot it. He said, "Come on, man, you're not going to kill a rabbit while we're moving." A couple of rabbits dart across the left. And, of course, I'm not going to shoot across my brother. Then one pops off to the right, and I fire. Nate says, "You didn't hit that."

But we pull up to where I shot, and this rabbit is dead, with a bullet hole in it. I shot a rabbit on the run. With a pistol. While holding on tight in the back of a moving four-wheeler. I freaking Doc Holliday'd this motherfucker. It made the hunt for me. So we pick it up and take it back to the camp. If I hadn't had a witness, I wouldn't have told anybody about it. No one would have believed me. But in Cajun country, if you do something crazy and you've got a witness, it's pretty much gold.

So, I take this rabbit and process him down. I took half a pack of bacon, whatever tomato product we had around, seared the rabbit, and cooked it down with the bacon and tomato over the fire.

(I guess we eat better than most folks at hunting camps now. But growing up, we'd make a feast of a loaf of white bread and Vienna sausages. We called them monkey dicks. I remember when they came out with smoked Vienna sausages and thinking, *Heyyyy, these are something special.* Now we bring artisanal cheese and oysters.)

But I didn't stop with just the rabbit stew with this prize kill. I stretched the skin out on a piece of plywood I found lying on the side of the camp, and tacked it up. I salted the skin and cured it with urine. You read that right. Urine, urea, when concentrated down, is a great curing agent for skins. It's what the Romans did. The expression "piss poor"? Legend has it, it refers to people who didn't have a bucket to piss in. People would sell their urine to places that cured hides, and if they couldn't collect their urine, they didn't have a way to sell it. So, I cut off the top of a beer can, peed in it, and put it on the fire to reduce down. (Ever been to the men's room at a football stadium in the late summer heat in south Louisiana? That's what it smelled like cooking over the fire.)

I found an old paintbrush and painted the reduced piss on the skin. I propped the plywood up next to the fire for some ambient heat overnight. The next morning, the hide was hard. When I got back home, I rubbed it with grapeseed oil to supple it up. Then, I went and got a dollar-store purse, cut the faux-hide off, and hot-glued my home-cured rabbit hide to the side. A little more Cajun engineering. And then I gave it to Amanda as a present.

We still have that purse, though I don't think Amanda ever took it out in public.

SMOKED DUCK GUMBO

We always make this gumbo after a good duck hunt. And even though you can make the recipe with farmed duck, wild is better. Of course, everything is better wild: ducks, frogs, women. We make it with two ducks, but if you've got more, multiply the recipe. It depends on how good of a shot you are—and how hungry. | *Serves 8 to 10*

Legs, thighs, necks, gizzards, and hearts of 2 ducks, with skin still on

3 teaspoons kosher salt, divided

2 teaspoons ground black pepper, divided

7 tablespoons grapeseed oil, divided

6 tablespoons all-purpose flour

1 large onion, finely diced

1 red bell pepper, finely diced

2 ribs celery, finely diced

10 cloves garlic, minced

1 (12-ounce) bottle dark beer (I use porter)

10 cups duck stock (page 13)

2 teaspoons smoked paprika

½ teaspoon cayenne pepper

1 teaspoon ground black pepper

5 bay leaves

1 pound smoked chorizo links (or other spicy pork sausage), sliced lengthwise and then cut into ¼-inch-thick half-moons (I use chaurice, the Cajun version of chorizo, but you won't find that outside of south Louisiana.)

Everyday Rice (page 17), for serving

EQUIPMENT
Smoker (optional, see Notes)

Notes: Don't use duck breasts here. While the gumbo is cooking, use the breasts to make the Ducks in the Pig Pen (page 207).

Let's say you don't have a smoker: You can season the duck parts and then roast them in a 400°F oven for about 35 minutes, until the skin is browned and starting to get crispy. It won't be smoky, but it will be delicious. If you roast it, deglaze the pan with an extra ¼ cup of dark beer and toss in with the duck stock.

› Preheat the smoker to 225°F.

› Put all the duck parts in a large mixing bowl. Sprinkle with 2 teaspoons of the salt, 1 teaspoon of the black pepper, and 1 tablespoon of the grapeseed oil. Toss it all together with your hands to make sure all the duck pieces are seasoned. Place the duck in the smoker and smoke for 1 hour, until the skin is browned and has a nice char; the duck parts should look like barbecue chicken when done.

› In a large Dutch oven over medium heat, make a dark roux (page 10), using the remaining 6 tablespoons grapeseed oil and the flour. When it's the color of milk chocolate, about 45 minutes, add the onion, bell pepper, and celery and sweat for 3 minutes, stirring occasionally. Add the garlic and cook for another minute, stirring occasionally. Add the beer to deglaze

the roux-and-vegetable mixture. Stir immediately and often, scraping up any browned bits from the bottom of the pan, until the mixture comes to a simmer.

› Add the duck stock, paprika, cayenne, bay leaves, and remaining 1 teaspoon salt and 1 teaspoon black pepper. Stir and add the chorizo chunks and smoked duck. Increase the heat to medium-high to bring it back up to a simmer, stirring frequently with a wooden spoon and scraping the bottom of the pot. Once it's back to a simmer, reduce the heat to low and cook uncovered for 2 hours, or until meat is falling off the bone.

› Serve over rice. It's even better the next day, and it freezes well. (That said, I've never actually frozen gumbo because there's never any left.)

DUCKS IN THE PIG PEN
(GRILLED BACON-WRAPPED DUCK BREASTS)

This is easily my favorite preparation of wild duck breasts. Wild ducks don't have a lot of meat on their legs, so they aren't worth grilling (but they're good for stock and gumbo). But the breast is always good, even from a small duck. And it would be a shame to waste good duck breasts by putting them in gumbo. So while you're at the camp and you've got the gumbo cooking with all the other parts, make yourself this snack with the breasts. | *Serves 4*

- 4 (4-ounce) skinless duck breasts (from 2 medium-size ducks)
- 1 tablespoon kosher salt
- 1½ teaspoons ground black pepper
- 1 jalapeño, seeded and split lengthwise into quarters
- 8 slices bacon

EQUIPMENT
- 8 wooden skewers, soaked in water for 10 minutes

Note: This is the one time I do not recommend thick-cut bacon. By the time it cooks, the duck breast will be overdone and dry. Use the regular thin grocery-store slices instead.

› Preheat the grill to medium (around 400°F).

› Season the duck breasts with the salt and pepper, equal amounts on both sides. With a boning knife or a thin paring knife, make a slice all the way through the middle of a breast, creating a pocket through the length of the breast. (Imagine the duck breast is an iPhone lying flat. Place the knife at the bottom where the charger would go and pierce straight through the duck breast to the other side.) Shove the quartered piece of jalapeño into the pocket. Lay two pieces of bacon side by side lengthwise on a cutting board. Place a duck breast at the bottom end of the bacon, with the jalapeño pocket perpendicular to the bacon. Roll the duck breast up in the bacon slices. Secure the bacon in place with two skewers, one per piece of bacon. Repeat with each duck breast.

› Place the bacon-wrapped duck breasts on the grill and cook for 3 to 4 minutes on each side, until the internal temperature is 125°F for medium. Pull off the grill and let rest 1 minute. Remove the skewers, slice each breast into ½-inch-thick medallions, and serve. Just pop 'em in your mouth like meat candy.

• CAJUN GAMES •

CHICKEN

This is real archaic. You take your pocketknife—
every Cajun has one—and you stand with your
legs apart. Your buddy stands several feet away
with his legs apart. You throw your pocketknife
down in between the other person's legs. It sticks
in the ground. Wherever it stuck, you move your
closest leg to that spot. You go back and forth,
steadily moving your feet in. The first person to
move their foot away when the knife is thrown,
loses. He's the chicken.

I've seen people take knives in the foot. I
never have, surprisingly. But I'm always the
one instigating the game. I'm good at throwing
and I've got a sharp pocketknife. And I'll go
straight at your foot right off the bat because I
want to make you flinch—I want to win. Ha!
You're playing with a psychopath.

PERSISTENCE

One time my dad went duck hunting with his brother Robert, his brother Peter, and my paw paw. Daddy and Uncle Peter were riding in a canoe being pulled through the Atchafalaya River in a bass boat by Uncle Robert and Paw Paw. It was 3 o'clock in the morning and only 40°F. They were in the canoe with waders, guns, decoys, the whole nine yards. The river was running a half knot across. And they had a hand signal system to indicate whether to speed up or slow down. They were moving along and doing pretty good when all of a sudden another boat came by and they caught the wake. They motioned for the pull boat to stop. But Paw Paw and Uncle Robert thought they meant to gas it. So they throttled it. The canoe got off to the side in the wake and flipped over.

Daddy couldn't see Peter. It was dark and cold. He'd lost the light on the boat and thought, "They've left us." All of a sudden he saw Peter pop up from beneath the canoe. Daddy was in the water with a child's life jacket tied around his neck. He was struggling. He wasn't even swimming, just running in place in the water. Peter swam over and knocked him and said, "Swim, you idiot." So they swam, and the boat finally came around to pick them up. Guns, decoys, wallet, everything—gone.

And like true sportsmen, they changed their clothes and went right back out.

BROWN-SUGAR-AND-SOY GLAZED ROAST DUCK

We bag a lot of mallards when hunting in this neck of the woods, so I cook them more than other kinds of duck. But you can make this recipe with any duck of a decent size. To serve, I take the breasts and legs completely off the carcass, then cut the breasts into ½-inch slices and separate the thighs from the legs and serve them whole. Everyone then fights over the wings and neck. It's so good you'll be chewing on the ass of the carcass. | *Serves 4*

- 2 cups plus 2 tablespoons brown sugar, divided
- 2 cups plus 1 tablespoon kosher salt, divided
- ¼ cup toasted whole black peppercorns
- 8 bay leaves
- Grated zest and juice of 4 large navel oranges
- 2 (12-ounce) bottles amber-style beer
- 3 quarts water
- Enough ice water (about 21 cups) to equal 3 gallons after simmering the brine mixture
- 1 large (2½-pound) Peking duck (or a wild mallard if you can get one), cleaned
- 1 tablespoon finely ground black pepper
- 2 tablespoons soy sauce (not reduced-sodium)

EQUIPMENT

- 4-gallon (or larger) food-safe container (you can get one at a restaurant supply store or online) or small cooler

BRINE THE DUCK

› Combine the 2 cups brown sugar, the 2 cups salt, peppercorns, bay leaves, orange zest and juice, beer, and water in a large stockpot. Bring to a boil over high heat, then reduce the heat to low and simmer for 20 minutes.

› Put the brine in the 4-gallon container or cooler, and add enough ice water to measure *exactly* 3 gallons. (It's important to keep the salt-to-water ratio for brines. You've already got the salt, so the amount of ice water you need to add will vary according to how much liquid you lost when boiling the brine.) Dunk the duck in the brine and refrigerate for 24 hours, stirring once halfway through. To stir, I just grab the duck and give it a good twist back and forth.

› After 24 hours and when you're ready to cook (if the duck brines a little longer, that's okay), remove the duck from brine and pat dry with paper towels, both the skin and inside the cavity. Let sit out for 30 minutes to come to room temperature.

ROAST THE DUCK

› Preheat the oven to 325°F.

› In a small bowl, mix the 2 tablespoons brown sugar, 1 tablespoon salt, the ground black pepper, and soy sauce. Rub the skin and inside the cavity of the duck with the mixture, using all of it.

› Place the duck, breast-side up, in a 9 x 13-inch baking dish. Roast for two hours. Cover with aluminum foil and place back in oven and roast for an additional 1 hour and 30 minutes. You'll know the duck is done when you pull on the back leg and it starts to come loose.

› Let the duck rest, still wrapped in foil, for 10 minutes. Remove the duck from the pan. Pour the fat and jus from the roasting pan into a bowl, and skim the fat, reserving the jus. Slice the duck, spoon the jus over the meat, and serve.

DOC HOLLIDAY BACON-TOMATO BRAISED RABBIT

This bacon-tomato braised rabbit was born out of hunger and Cajun resourcefulness. It was the last day of the hunt, we'd about gone through all the groceries we'd brought, and I'd just shot a rabbit. How'd you kill the rabbit, you ask? Well, I was hunting for deer. (For the whole story, see page 202.)

This dish is the product of what we had on hand. Wild rabbit always needs added fat, so I grabbed some bacon. We didn't have any tomatoes, but we had fresh salsa, so that went in. (I still prefer salsa in it over fresh tomatoes.) The finished product is like a ragu with a thick tomato gravy. At the camp, we eat it right out of the pan. But you can serve it over grits, rice, or even a can of black-eyed peas. | *Serves 4*

- 1 (2½-pound) rabbit, head off, dressed (no skin, no guts except heart, liver, and kidneys if you have them)
- 2 tablespoons grapeseed oil, divided
- 2 teaspoons kosher salt
- 1 teaspoon ground black pepper
- 8 ounces thick-cut bacon, cut into squares
- 1 large onion, medium diced
- 6 cloves garlic, peeled and crushed
- 3 bay leaves
- 2 anchovy filets, smashed
- 1 cup fresh salsa (the good pico de gallo kind, not jarred)
- 1 (12-ounce) bottle amber-style beer
- ½ cup water

› Rub the rabbit down with 1 tablespoon of the grapeseed oil and season generously with the salt and pepper.

› Heat a Dutch oven and 1 tablespoon oil over medium heat for about 2 minutes, until it's hot. Sear the rabbit hard for 2 minutes on each side. (If you're using the organs, leave them in the rabbit cavity while you sear.) Remove the rabbit. Add the bacon and onion and sweat for 2 to 4 minutes, stirring occasionally, until the bacon starts to render and the onions begin to soften. Add the garlic and bay leaves and sweat for another minute, stirring occasionally. Stir in the anchovies and salsa and bring to a simmer. Add the beer and water and give it a good stir. Add the rabbit. Bring to a simmer and cover with lid slightly ajar.

› Simmer for 1 hour, then flip the rabbit. Return lid (still askew) and simmer for another hour and 20 minutes, until the rabbit is fork tender. Serve that bad boy.

HASENPFEFFER
(BLACK PEPPER RABBIT WITH SHERRY LENTILS)

This recipe wasn't actually born at the hunt camp. I just really wanted to make a rabbit dish called *Hasenpfeffer* because I remember it from my Bugs Bunny–watching years. In one cartoon, there was a king who wanted the royal cook (played by Yosemite Sam) to prepare *Hasenpfeffer*—which literally means "pepper rabbit." Look out, Bugs. The cook looked up the recipe in this big old book and the name was written large across the top. I've been curious about it ever since. I tried to find some old, authentic recipes for it but struck out. So I put my demented curiosity to use and imagined how that cartoon cook might have prepared it—and voilà! | *Serves 4*

4 bone-in rabbit hind legs

2 teaspoons ground black pepper

1½ teaspoons kosher salt

1 tablespoon grapeseed oil

1 large onion, julienned or thinly sliced

2 large carrots, peeled and diced

2 ribs celery, diced

10 cloves garlic, thinly sliced

2 large knobs fresh ginger (about 2 ounces), sliced into ¼-inch-thick slices

½ cup bourbon

2 cups chicken stock (page 12 or store-bought)

Sherry Lentils (recipe follows) or Everyday Rice (page 17), for serving

› Preheat the oven to 350°F. Generously season the rabbit with the black pepper and salt.

› In a large straight-sided sauté pan, heat the oil over high heat until it's just starting to smoke (not pluming like Mt. Vesuvius, but just starting to smoke), about 2 minutes. Add the rabbit legs and sear for 2 minutes on each side. Transfer the rabbit to a casserole/baking dish just large enough to fit the legs snugly, about 9 x 13 inches.

› Add the onion, carrots, celery, garlic, and ginger to the sauté pan, reduce the heat to medium, and cook for 2 minutes, stirring occasionally, until beginning to soften.

› Add the bourbon (it should not ignite) and scrape with a wooden spoon to deglaze the pan. Remove from the heat as soon as the browned bits on the bottom of the pan have fully released.

› Spoon the bourbon-vegetable mixture evenly on top of the rabbit and gently tamp it down. Pour the stock over the rabbit and vegetables. Cover the dish with a lid or wrap tightly with aluminum foil. Bake for 2 hours and 20 minutes, until the liquid is brothy, but not soupy.

› Remove from the oven and uncover. Remove the pieces of ginger. Serve in bowls over sherry lentils or rice.

SHERRY LENTILS

I imagine *Hasenpfeffer* as a regal dish from the days of olde. It makes me want to drink my wine out of a proper glass, not straight out of the bottle. It makes me want to bust out the nice silverware and the good napkins. So it needs a special side dish. I didn't grow up eating lentils—just every other bean under the sun—so Sherry Lentils just sounds elegant to me.

2 tablespoons unsalted butter	½ teaspoon crushed red pepper flakes	1 pound whole lentils (I prefer black, but any will do)
1 carrot, peeled and finely diced	1 quart veal stock (page 13); chicken stock (page 12) will also work	1 tablespoon sherry vinegar (can substitute red wine vinegar, but then you'd have Red Wine Lentils)
1 onion, finely diced	1 tablespoon kosher salt	
1 tablespoon chopped fresh thyme		

› In a large saucepot, melt the butter over medium heat. Add the carrot, onion, thyme, and pepper flakes and cook for 5 minutes, stirring occasionally, until the onions have browned slightly. Deglaze with the stock and add the salt. Add the lentils and stir. Bring up to a simmer over medium heat, then cover and reduce heat to maintain a low simmer.

› Cook for 20 minutes, until the lentils are slightly soft and just cooked through—a little al dente. If you're in doubt, just know it's better to overcook than undercook lentils. Stir in the sherry vinegar, remove from the heat, and serve.

SMOKED TURKEY LEGS

I don't love turkey, but I can get down with smoked turkey legs. They're the perfect outdoor barbecue food and practically beg to be brought to a tailgate. And there is no way to eat one without getting it all over your face and getting your hands dirty. Try it with a bunch of kids. It's fun to watch them try and take down something that's the size of their own legs. | *Serves 4*

4 (1-pound) turkey legs (these are the big boys)

25 cloves garlic, minced

6 tablespoons mustard powder

6 tablespoons smoked paprika

6 tablespoons ground black pepper

3½ tablespoons kosher salt

EQUIPMENT
Smoker (optional)

› Preheat the smoker (or oven) to 250°F. You can make these in the oven if you need to, but the smoker is where it's at. Personally, if I didn't have a smoker, I wouldn't even bother.

› Score the turkey legs: On the meatier side of each leg, make three slices into the flesh, about an inch apart, cutting all the way down to the bone. Cut two more slashes on the other side, staggering between the other slashes. (That is, do not cut a ring all the way around the bone.) This will expose more turkey meat to the spice rub.

› In a small mixing bowl, combine the garlic, mustard, paprika, pepper, and salt. I like to mix it with my hand, really agitate it. Divide this mixture into 4 equal piles. Rub a pile well into each turkey leg, making sure each leg is well covered and the spices get deep into the cuts and crevices.

› Place the seasoned turkey legs in the smoker (or oven) and smoke (or bake) for 2 hours, or until the internal temperature is 155°F. Let cool for about 5 minutes. Eat like the barbarian you are.

VENISON WITH
CARAMELIZED ONION BARLEY, HORSERADISH CREAM, AND JAM

Strictly speaking, this isn't a Cajun dish. But you could serve it to a Cajun and they wouldn't notice. Cajuns don't care about rules and what is or isn't Cajun. So what if this is actually inspired by a Viking dish I cooked on *Top Chef*? We hunt deer and eat deer. And this is delicious. You can also make it with beef tenderloins if you're just not into the whole eating-Bambi thing. | *Serves 4*

2 (1-pound) venison loins, trimmed of all sinew (or 2 beef tenderloins)

6 teaspoons kosher salt

4 tablespoons Venison Spice (recipe follows)

4 tablespoons unsalted butter

½ cup good-quality jam (your choice), for serving

Horseradish Cream (recipe follows), for serving

Caramelized Onion Barley (recipe follows), for serving

› This venison is going to be very rare—bloody rare. But venison is so lean, if you cook it much past rare it will be overdone, dry, and tough.

› Twenty minutes before you start cooking, pull the venison from the fridge and let it come up to room

temperature. After 15 minutes, season each side of each loin with 1½ teaspoons kosher salt and 1 tablespoon venison spice. The loin should look like it has a spice crust. Let the seasoned loin rest for the additional 5 minutes.

› If your large skillet won't hold both loins without crowding, cook them individually—either simultaneously in separate skillets, or one after the other. In each of two large skillets (if cooking in batches), heat 2 tablespoons butter on medium heat for 3 to 4 minutes, until browned. (Heat all 4 tablespoons butter in one large skillet if cooking in one batch.) Place the venison loin in the skillet and give the pan a shake to make sure the fat is distributed under and around the meat. Sear the meat on one side for 3 minutes, then flip. Sear for an additional 3 minutes, moving it around in the pan a couple of times to make sure the venison comes fully in contact with the melted butter. Remove from the heat. Reserve the pan drippings and butter.

› Rest the venison for 1 minute. Slice into ½-inch slices and sprinkle with a little kosher salt. Arrange on a platter and spoon jam on top of the slices. Pour leftover brown butter from the pan over the jam. Serve with the Horseradish Cream and Caramelized Onion Barley.

VENISON SPICE

Makes 6 tablespoons

2 tablespoons whole black peppercorns

2 tablespoons whole yellow mustard seeds

2 tablespoons whole cumin seeds

› Combine all the spices and toast in a dry skillet over medium-low heat until aromatic. Remove from the heat and let cool to room temperature. With a mortar and pestle or a spice grinder, finely grind the toasted spices.

HORSERADISH CREAM

I put this shit on everything, from baked potatoes to French fries to roasted vegetables. So don't worry about this recipe making more than you need for the venison—put the rest in the fridge and use it the next day. | *Makes a generous ½ cup*

6 tablespoons sour cream

¼ cup hot (spicy) prepared horseradish

¼ teaspoon Venison Spice (recipe above)

½ teaspoon kosher salt

› Whisk to combine all ingredients.

CARAMELIZED ONION BARLEY

This barley dish was one I created on *Top Chef* to go with the Viking venison dish. Apparently Vikings ate like Cajuns: a lot of meat, few vegetables, and some grains. I'd never cooked barley before, but I have a little chef trick that puts me above a lot of others when I don't know how to cook something: I read the back of the package. You should see how well that works. And I learned that ultimately you cook barley like grits. I was home-free then. | *Serves 4*

1 tablespoon neutral vegetable oil, like canola or grapeseed

1 large sweet onion (I like Vidalia or red), thinly sliced

Kosher salt

3 cups veal or chicken stock (pages 12–13 or store-bought)

1 teaspoon mustard powder

1 teaspoon ground cumin

1 teaspoon ground black pepper

1 cup pearled barley

2 tablespoons unsalted butter

› In a medium saucepan, heat the oil over high heat until it just begins to smoke. Add the onions and a pinch of salt and stir. Continue stirring every 30 seconds for about 5 minutes, until the onions start to lightly caramelize. Reduce the heat to low and continue to cook for another 10 minutes, stirring once every minute, until the onions are golden brown but not burnt.

› Add the stock, mustard, cumin, black pepper, 2 teaspoons salt, and the barley and bring to a simmer, stirring once. Cover and simmer for 35 minutes, until barley is cooked all the way through and is not crunchy. Remove from the heat and let rest for 5 minutes. Uncover and stir in the butter. Serve.

PASTA IN PURGATORY

At the hunt camp, where refrigeration usually just means an ice chest, you need easy food options. There, Purgatory is my go-to sauce. It's my backwoods rendition of the classic Italian or Middle Eastern spicy tomato sauce. I serve it with pasta. I poach eggs in it for breakfast. I dilute it to braise meats. You can even make pizza with it if you're a bougie fucker who makes pizza at a hunt camp. If you were in a real bind, you could warm it up in a coffee cup and eat it as a snack with a piece of white bread. And it jars well, so if you're into canning you can have some on hand year-round. | *Serves 4*

2 teaspoons grapeseed oil

1 large onion, finely diced

1 pound smoked sausage links, diced

1 cup minced garlic (about 65 cloves)

1 cup tomato paste (1½ six-ounce cans)

4 large tomatoes, cored and diced

1 teaspoon smoked paprika

4 cups chicken stock (page 12 or store-bought)

2 teaspoons Isaac's Pickled Pepper Paste of Pain (page 21) or hot sauce

1 teaspoon kosher salt

1 teaspoon ground black pepper

1 pound cooked pasta, for serving

› Heat the oil in a large Dutch oven over medium heat for about 2 minutes, until shimmering. Add the onion and sausage and cook for 4 minutes, stirring occasionally. Add the garlic and cook for another minute, stirring occasionally. Stir in the tomato paste and cook for about 2 minutes, until it caramelizes and begins to stick to the bottom of the pot. Add the diced tomatoes, making sure to stir the bottom of the pot with a wooden spoon to scrape the caramelized tomato paste off the bottom.

Add the stock, pepper paste, smoked paprika, salt, and pepper, stirring all together well. Keep the heat on medium and let the sauce slowly come up to a simmer. Give it a stir. Reduce the heat to low and continue to simmer, uncovered, for 1 hour. It should be loose like a soup when you start and as it cooks down over the hour, the end result will be chunky and thick like jarred tomato sauce.

› Serve over cooked pasta.

THREE MORE WAYS TO GET STUCK IN PURGATORY

EGGS IN PURGATORY

› Make the sauce, crack some whole eggs into it, and put the whole pan in a 375°F oven. Bake for about 10 minutes, until the whites are set and the yolks are still runny.

PURGATORY CHILI

› Season 1 pound lean ground beef with 2 teaspoons salt and 1 teaspoon pepper. In a large sauté pan, heat 1 tablespoon vegetable oil over medium heat. Once the oil starts to smoke, add the beef and brown hard for 8 to 10 minutes. Drain the fat from the pan and add 1 cup chicken or veal stock and 2 cups Purgatory Sauce. Cover and simmer for 45 minutes.

Serve with corn chips and big fistfuls of your favorite melty cheese.

EVIL CHICKEN THIGHS IN PURGATORY

> Preheat oven to 350°F. Season 4 chicken thighs with salt and pepper. Brown them in 1 tablespoon vegetable oil in an ovenproof pan over medium-high heat, 2 minutes on each side. Remove the chicken from the pan and deglaze with 1½ cups chicken stock. Stir 1½ cups Purgatory Sauce into the stock. Add the thighs back and heat until the sauce simmers. Cover and bake in oven for 1 hour 15 minutes, until thighs are fork tender. Remove and rest for 10 minutes. Serve.

LOUISIANA DITCH CHICKEN
(FRIED FROG LEGS)

These are Cajun chicken wings—which means they're really frog legs. I'm from Rayne, Louisiana, the Frog Capital of the World. There's a frog festival every year, where they have tadpole races (really toddlers crawling to their mothers) and crown a Frog Queen. I grew up catching frogs in my backyard, either gigging them (hitting them with a spring-loaded hook on the end of a stick), catching them by hand, or shooting them with a .22. Yeah, we'd go in the backyard and shoot 'em. No, shooting them doesn't blow them to smithereens. These are full-sized Louisiana bullfrogs. Them fuckers get big.

I get Louisiana frog legs through a local seafood company, but you can often find them at Asian markets. I only buy them pre-cleaned, because cleaning frogs is a hellacious process. Don't bother with it. If you can't find frog legs, don't worry your pretty little head: This recipe also works with chicken wing drumettes. | *Serves 6*

- 2 quarts full-fat buttermilk (none of that low-fat nonsense—it's for flavor, people)
- 2 tablespoons hot sauce
- 4 tablespoons paprika, divided
- 1 teaspoon celery salt
- 2 tablespoons kosher salt
- 1 teaspoon ground black pepper
- 24 frog legs (from 12 frogs); or 24 chicken wing drumettes
- 2 quarts peanut oil
- 8 cups all-purpose flour
- ¼ cup popcorn salt
- 2 tablespoons garlic powder
- 3 tablespoons onion powder
- 2 tablespoons ground white pepper

› In a large bowl, whisk together the buttermilk, hot sauce, 1 tablespoon of the paprika, the celery salt, kosher salt, and black pepper. Submerge the frog legs in the buttermilk mixture and mix well until the legs are coated. Cover and put the bowl in the fridge. Let sit for 12 to 24 hours to brine.

› In a deep-sided cast iron skillet, Dutch oven, or deep fryer set over high heat, heat the peanut oil to 350°F. It should be about 1½ inches deep, but more oil is better than less when frying.

› In a mixing bowl, whisk the flour with the remaining 3 tablespoons paprika, the popcorn salt, garlic powder, onion powder, and white pepper.

› Remove one-third of the frog legs from the brine (for 24 legs, I do eight at a time, dredging and frying in three batches). Dredge them in the seasoned flour, ensuring each leg is fully covered. Place the floured frog legs in the hot oil—they should be fully submerged—and cook for 3 to 4 minutes, until golden brown. Remove the frog legs from oil and drain on paper towels. Repeat until all legs are cooked, letting the oil come back up to temperature (350°F) between batches.

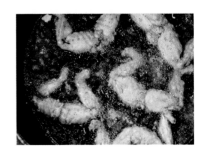

FROG GIGGIN'

To catch frogs, you go out at night with a headlight and a frog giggin' stick, which is essentially a spring-loaded claw on the end of a broomstick or old shovel handle. You open the claw manually, like a mini bear trap, 'til it's open and taut. There's a little release button, so when you hit something, it snaps shut. It really hurts when your older brother hits you with that shit in the leg. It'll take your shoe off. Or you can just grab the frogs by hand. They're big ole suckers, but they don't bite. Or you can just shoot them with a .22.

But really if you want frogs, just hustle up some kids to go find them for you. You'll rarely see adults heading out just to get frogs. It's far more likely that they're hunting something else at night (gator trapping, nutria hunting), and grabbed a few frogs on the side.

HOPPER STEW

The legs are the primo part of the frog. No one really saves frog backs—they're the frog by-product—so they're the first thing to get cooked and fed to a hungry country crowd. This rustic stew, enriched with delicious pork fat, is also called a *sauce piquant*, and is the perfect way to cook backs. You won't eat these very ceremoniously—it's not like a Frenchman delicately nibbling on a frog. You break open the back and pick the bones—the backwoods way. If you can't get your hands on frog backs, chicken thighs will also work. | *Serves 6*

- 2 pounds frog backs, from about 12 frogs (or 2 pounds bone-in chicken thighs)
- 1 teaspoon cayenne pepper, divided
- 3 teaspoons kosher salt, divided

- 2 teaspoons ground black pepper
- 2 tablespoons all-purpose flour
- 2 tablespoons grapeseed oil
- 6 ounces fatty pork belly, finely diced or ground
- 1 small onion, finely diced
- 2 ribs celery, finely diced

- 1 red bell pepper, finely diced
- 8 cloves garlic, minced
- 1 (12-ounce) bottle amber-style beer
- 1½ cups water
- ¼ cup tomato paste
- Everyday Rice (page 17), for serving

Note: For the pork belly, you can substitute fatback or even use a piece of fatty pork shoulder. I avoid bacon here because I don't want a smoky flavor in the stew.

› Season the frog backs with ½ teaspoon of the cayenne, 2 teaspoons of the salt, and the black pepper. Dust the backs with the flour (sprinkle the flour over them, as you would with salt).

› Take out a large sauté pan that's big enough to fit all the frog backs without touching. (If you don't have a pan that's big enough, you can cook them in batches.) Add the oil and heat over medium heat until it starts to shimmer, about 2 minutes. Right as it begins to smoke, add the frog backs, spreading them out evenly in the pan. Cook over medium heat for 2 to 3 minutes on each side, until falling apart. Remove the frog backs and reserve.

› In the same pan, over medium heat, add the pork belly. You'll need to break it up with a wooden spoon—it likes to stick together. Add the onion, celery, and bell pepper. Stir together and cook for 3 minutes, regularly scraping

the bottom of the pan with a wooden spoon. Add the garlic and cook for 1 minute, stirring constantly. Add the beer and stir to scrape up the browned bits from the pan. Allow to come to a simmer to remove most of the alcohol. Add the water, tomato paste, and remaining 1 teaspoon salt and ½ teaspoon cayenne and stir. Return to a simmer.

› Once it's simmering, add the frog backs back to the pan with the gravy. Reduce the heat to low and simmer, uncovered, for 1 hour. Stir them very gently about halfway through. As they cook over a low simmer, the frog backs will become very delicate, so be careful when you stir that they don't fall apart.

› To serve, gently ladle 2 to 3 frog backs over white rice and add a generous scoop of gravy.

ACKNOWLEDGMENTS

Jennifer V. Cole, for going inside my head and making it out successfully.

Denny Culbert, for being up for the adventure and making my food look less brown.

Poppy and Ivy Toups, for forcing us to get our act together.

My parents, Brent and Esther Toups, for an unmatched upbringing full of culinary adventures. Steve and Janis Floyd, for raising my greatest muse and soulmate.

My grandparents, for their individual and unique inspiration.

Emeril Lagasse, for making me the chef I am today.

Jason and Jamie Toups, Celeste and Jim Babineaux, Nathaniel Toups, Stephen and Melissa Floyd, Marty and Diane Floyd, Mike Szczerban and the entire Little, Brown team, David Hale Smith, Larry Nguyen, Josh Wilkins, David Barbeau, Mario Reyes, Courtney Hellenschmidt, Seamus Rozycki, Jason Lambert, Christine Tran, Neal Swidler, Drew Knoll, Spencer Minch, Anthony Scanio, Wilfredo Avalar, Darren Chabert, David Slater, Chris Wilson, Rémy Robert, Amelia Singleton, Kyle and Peggy Johnston, Kat Kinsman, Joe Vidrine, Joel Savoy, David McClevey, and every single person that has supported us along the way. Thank you.

—Isaac Toups

My parents, Sellers and Julia Cole, for supporting all of my dreams and giving me an anchor for my peripatetic ways.

Prentiss and Jeremy Cole, for being the best brothers I could have ever hoped for.

Lily Belle, Katelyn, Keaton, Logan, Sam, and Parker, for always choosing adventure.

My grandparents, Clyde and Vashti Muse and Everett and Jane Cole.

My constantly on-call texting brigade—Bill Addison, Simone Reggie, Kat Kinsman—for letting me spill my guts and keeping me going.

Maria Flavia Mammana (and Daniele, Giacomo, and Maria Roberta), for allowing me to take over the dining room table in Catania to actually write this book.

Miguel Castro, mi hermano. The Breakfast Club (SA, RM, KM, PVW, and PH) for unwavering support and perfectly timed laughs. Keri Bernsen Cole, Kathryn Barger Cole, Alana Jacobs Duncanson, Brent and Caroline Rosen, Nejla Orgen, Katya Musacchio, Nancy Novogrod, Mario Mercado, John Alex Floyd, Warner McGowin, Lindsay Bierman, Rachel Hardage Barrett, Sid Evans, Scott Mowbray, Jim Baker, Dana Cowin, Taylor Bruce, Nellah McGough, Rémy Robert, Mike Szczerban, Nicky Guerreiro, Deri Reed, and the rest of the Little, Brown team.

And Isaac and Amanda, for taking me on this wild ride and making me part of the family.

—Jennifer V. Cole

INDEX

ABOUT THE AUTHORS

Chef Isaac Toups, a James Beard Award nominee for Best Chef of the South and Bravo TV's *Top Chef* season 13 Fan Favorite, exemplifies the new guard of Cajun chefs. He is the chef/owner of Toups' Meatery and Toups South in New Orleans. With family roots in southern Louisiana that span more than 300 years, Toups' culinary style was influenced by both of his grandmothers and his upbringing with days spent hunting, fishing, and connecting with his surroundings. His unique combination of childhood roots, along with honing his skills in some of New Orleans' most acclaimed restaurants—including a decade of fine dining experience in Emeril Lagasse's New Orleans kitchens—gives the critically acclaimed chef a cutting edge that is unrivaled.

Jennifer V. Cole spent nearly a decade getting to know the intricacies of the South at *Southern Living* magazine, where she served as deputy editor and where her annual restaurant lists were considered the final word on where to eat in the region. Her writing appears widely in other publications, including *Food & Wine, Garden & Gun*, and Wildsam Field Guides. A native of Mississippi, she spent eight years in New York City, where she annually had live crawfish flown up for her birthday boil—she purged them in her bathtub, to the chagrin of her roommates. She now lives as a vagabond, continuously traveling the world.